How to Be Happier Day by Day

How to Be Happier Day by Day

A Year of Mindful Actions

Alan Epstein, Ph.D.

Viking

VIKING
Published by the Penguin Group
Viking Penguin, a division of Penguin Books USA Inc.,
375 Hudson Street, New York, New York 10014, U.S.A.
Penguin Books Ltd, 27 Wrights Lane,
London W8 5TZ, England
Penguin Books Australia Ltd, Ringwood,
Victoria, Australia
Penguin Books Canada Ltd, 10 Alcorn Avenue, Suite 300,
Toronto, Ontario, Canada M4V 3B2
Penguin Books (N.Z.) Ltd, 182–190 Wairau Road,
Auckland 10, New Zealand

Penguin Books Ltd, Registered Offices:
Harmondsworth, Middlesex, England

First published in 1993 by Viking Penguin,
a division of Penguin Books USA Inc.

1 3 5 7 9 10 8 6 4 2

Copyright © Alan Epstein, 1993
All rights reserved

LIBRARY OF CONGRESS CATALOGING IN PUBLICATION DATA
Epstein, Alan, 1949–
How to be happier day by day : a year of mindful actions. / Alan Epstein.
p. cm.
ISBN 0-670-84787-9
1. Happiness—Problems, exercises, etc. 2. Attention—Problems,
exercises, etc. 3. Awareness—Problems, exercises, etc. I. Title.
BF575.H27E77 1993
158'.1—dc20 92-495

Printed in the United States of America
Set in Century Book Condensed
Designed by Brian Mulligan

To my companions, Diane, Julian, and Elliott
To Steve, who showed me the way, and
To the memory of Ethan

Acknowledgments

There are a number of precious individuals who contributed mightily to this book.

Ivan Levison was an early and ardent supporter not only of this project but of the changes in my life that led—eventually—to this book being written. Our frequent lunches at "The Club" are truly the stuff of which legend—or comedy—is made.

Susan Page has been a constant source of guidance, support, and inspiration. Her thoughtful counsel has helped smooth the inevitable rough spots that every writer faces. Dorothy Wall's early critique of the manuscript was insightful at a time when this project was still a gleam in my eye.

Heartfelt thanks go to the following for their friendship, encouragement, and creative ideas: Lisa Gerber, Tom Markham, Barbra Markham, Gail Howe, JuliAnne Kaplan, Lawry Kaplan, Jodi Henry-Petty, Terry Petty, and Zack Edison. Steve Isaacs and Phil Jones were great sounding boards, especially for title suggestions, patiently considering every one of them.

I am extremely fortunate to be the recipient of the knowledge and expertise of the people at Viking Penguin. My editor, Pam Dorman, is a writer's dream—supportive, solicitous, constructively critical, and creative. Her sense of what makes a great book is incorporated into every page. Every conversation I have with Paris Wald reminds me that this project is in loving and mindful hands. And Cathy Hemming's enthusiastic backing is something I treasure.

My agent, Patti Breitman, recognized a good idea when she saw it, maintained unwavering belief in its success, especially when my ordinarily optimistic nature was tested, and continues to be a dear friend and trusted adviser. Linda Michaels has done an outstanding job representing this book to foreign publishers, and shares my love of Italy, to boot.

I cannot say enough about the lifelong love and support I have received from my parents, Litzi and Len Epstein, and brother, Perry Epstein, and the encouragement of my in-laws, Phyllis and Hank Ginsberg. Many people would consider themselves fortunate to have one wonderful family. I must be blessed, for I have two.

And finally, words certainly cannot describe the role played in my life by my wife and "true partner," Diane. Not only are many of the suggestions contained in this book straight out of her fertile, creative mind, her loving spirit suffuses the entire enterprise. She is my editor, coach, business partner, and guiding light. She is my biggest fan, and severest critic. Without her devotion and unwavering faith—both in me and in the universe—life would be much less rich than it is.

Contents

Introduction

Most of us want to be happy, or at least happier. We want to feel the joy associated with those rare moments when our happiness is so complete that there is nothing about the present moment we would change. But too often we look for happiness outside of ourselves—in the approval of others, the absolute control of our personal environments, and the constant infusion of new and better personal gadgets—and then wonder why life hasn't brought us the satisfaction we seek.

Happiness is not external; it is not a function of what one does or does not do. Happiness is in the *attitude* that one brings to everything one does. One, in effect, *creates* happiness. Siblings can and often do relate to the same family conditions in completely different ways. One can be ecstatic, the other perfectly miserable. Additionally, people of great means and privilege are not guaranteed happiness, while those who have less often live satisfying and fulfilling lives.

So if we create our own happiness, what should we be aiming toward? The answer: happiness is the fulfillment of our dreams, the accomplishment of what we set out to do, living our lives as we want to live them. There's no surprise here, really. Freud said as much at the beginning of the century. But it still leaves us with the question, "What do I *do?*"

The irony is that we fail to see how regularly we are already "doing it." Too often we see our "dreams" only in terms of our big, enduring, life dreams, and tend to overlook the little things we accomplish day in, day out. We neglect the fact that having our day run smoothly is the fulfillment of a wish—the wish, simply, to be more in control of our daily lives. Happiness, then, can reside in the carrying out of the myriad everyday tasks that we all take for granted, with one very small, but significant, difference. Outwardly, we may be doing what we always do, but inwardly, our entire being is immersed and engaged more fully in each and every action, a condition known as *mindfulness.*

People are happiest when they have either accomplished something—however small—that they originally considered a challenge, or when they allow themselves to see a familiar landscape in a new way. People who are generally happy do this all the time. They expose themselves to new experiences, which may or may not produce immediate pleasure or comfort. They often take risks. Unhappy people almost never do.

Many deceptively simple everyday projects can create happiness—like saying hello to everyone you meet, or eating only fresh foods, or exploring a nearby location for the first time. And familiar, routine tasks, such as taking a bath, visiting the public library, or writing a letter, can be fulfilling when performed with a different attitude.

It's through the blending of mindfulness and the taking of small risks that these mundane tasks are transformed into exciting challenges, which can then become the foundation of a life of happiness.

Mindfulness is a desirable, yet elusive, state. It is what turns ordinary experience into extraordinary experience. It is not only a conscious awareness of what one is doing, but also an embracing of the task in a way such that all distinction between the task and the person performing it is erased.

It is putting into alignment where one is and where one wants to be, so that no separation exists between the two.

Mindfulness implies having a purpose—the setting forth of a plan, big or small; it implies bringing one's entire being to the project—the merging of mind, body, and spirit; it implies total immersion—no distractions, diversions, deterrents, or halfhearted attempts.

When applied to the specific actions of everyday life, mindfulness can have a powerful impact on its quality. The simple task of asking someone for help can be a difficult, even terrifying, experience. But what if you were to focus your attention away from the fear of the actual request, and place it on some of the larger issues? What makes you want to do this particular job? Do you have an overall vision for getting it done? Why are you asking for help? Is it because you really can't do the job yourself, or because you simply want support and company? What do you intend to give in return for the help? What if you let your mind ponder these aspects of the project for a day or so until it came up with a list of three people to whom you could turn? The request for help would be easier, the chances of compliance greater, and the net effect of the entire exercise could be a feeling of accomplishment, enhancement, communication, reciprocity, and vitality.

The eventual result of mindfulness is a quantum leap forward in the quotient of one's happiness. The successful meeting of these small challenges adds up to something quite exceptional—a large measure of heightened self-awareness that is critical to sustained personal development, and, therefore, more happiness. Happiness is growth through the enlargement of one's comfort zone, the expansion of what one has attempted, and the self-confidence to attempt even more.

While this book contains no suggestions that will physically endanger you—like climbing Mount Everest or skydiving—the actions recommended might cause one's submerged feelings to be activated, which can lead to some discomfort. It is the unfortunate but indisputable truth that happiness often comes with a price. In this case it is the uneasiness one goes through in the process of becoming more mindful, the prerequisite of happiness. It is tantamount to a snake's shedding its skin in order to live.

How to Use This Book

How to Be Happier Day by Day

can be used in a variety of ways. You can:

1. follow each selection, day by day, as a systematic guide to becoming happier
2. skip suggestions
3. repeat ones that work well
4. take as many days as you need to carry out each suggestion
5. add variations that suit your personality
6. delete suggestions that don't feel right
7. carry the book with you, open it impulsively, and select a suggestion at random, or
8. organize a support group with your family, friends, or acquaintances, meet once a week, assign a suggestion to each member, and discuss it the following week

To use the book most systematically, I would suggest reading at least one week in advance, and deciding what you want to do and when you want to do it. Some of the suggestions—taking public transportation, for example—require planning. Some—like renting funny movies—can be done on the spur of the moment. Some projects—such as cleaning out your closets—require more than a day, while others—like sitting in a café—need no more than an hour. Don't feel constrained by the calendar dates; they are not critical. You can do any suggestion on any day. And some suggestions, like walking in the rain, obviously require cooperation from outside forces. A short essay at the end of each month will act, I hope, as a guidepost, explaining in a more conceptual way how the daily suggestions relate to both mindfulness and happiness.

Another way to capture the spirit of the book is to carry out the suggestions most contrary to the way you normally live your life. If you meticulously plan everything down to the last detail, then close your eyes, open the book, and do what it suggests on the day you open to. If your life is normally chaotic, with very little planning, then you may want to challenge yourself to follow the book as it is written, day by day, the effect being the creation of more order and awareness in and of your life.

Some of the suggestions here will stir up feelings that you might not want to face right away. Do not do what feels inappropriate to you, but do try to take some risks. The key to deeper enjoyment is expanding your repertoire of action, realizing that you are capable of a wider range of activities because you are actually carrying them out on a regular basis. The process is the same as starting a routine of physical exercise: it hurts at first, and then, as you do more of it, the pain goes away and both your body and your psyche feel the advantages.

You can even (heaven forbid!) read all the suggestions without attempting any of them. While you will derive less than the full benefit of this book, you will still have been introduced to a different way of looking at the world. But if you attempt and complete a great number of these tasks with a mindful attitude, your life will be a happier, more fulfilling, one. You will find that creating a life of happiness is not one large, overwhelming task, but rather a series of small, manageable steps.

How to Be
Happier
Day by Day

January

1 January, New Year's Day *Say hello to everyone you see.* Don't wait for others to acknowledge you—acknowledge them first. If you're doing this right, people you already know will be amazed at your heightened friendliness. Strangers will think you are an exceptionally warm person.

Smiling is great, too. If you're intimidated by someone's severe demeanor, smile at him, and try to see his response before turning away. In the final analysis, however, his reaction to your overt warmth is of no concern. Even if only one person returns your smile or hello today, consider your effort a major success. You'd be surprised at how many people you can affect simply by smiling at them.

2 January *Start a piggy bank.* If you want to be a traditionalist, use a ceramic, metal, or plastic pig, but any type of container will do.

It also doesn't matter whether you save pennies or all kinds of change. What's important is that you place the change in your piggy bank either at the beginning or the end of each day. Don't spend the money: Once it goes in it doesn't come out until you can't put any more in.

Starting a piggy bank provides concrete evidence of your ability to save, and to follow through and accomplish something long-term. If your piggy bank is an open tray or dish, you can observe the fruit of your determination. If you have a real piggy bank, pick it up from time to time and feel its weight.

When your piggy bank is full, put the change in wrappers, take the rolls to the bank, get bills, and buy something you'll really enjoy. You'll be amazed at how much extra money you have saved, and how satisfied you feel. Then start over tomorrow.

3 January *Go through all your papers and files at work or at home and make sure everything you need is at hand and everything you don't need ends up in its proper place.* If you really don't need it, throw it away. Hold on to only what you're sure you need, and be ruthless about getting rid of things that are old, out of date, or unimportant.

Getting rid of things you don't need is an essential part of making room in your life for new things. When your business and household affairs are in order—or at least under control—you'll marvel at how easy it is to get things done, and also to have a clear mind.

For instance, if you file papers immediately rather than letting them pile up, you'll spend less time looking for them and be less likely to lose or misplace them. When you cook, clean up as you go along. Throw out what you don't need and wash bowls and utensils in which you've prepared food as soon as you're finished with them. You'll have much less to do later.

Tasks you used to dread suddenly become pleasurable if you know exactly what you have to do, when you have to do it, where the tools are, and whom you have to ask to help you.

4 January   *Go through your old magazines and cut out all the pictures and words that appeal to you.* If you feel a picture or sentence represents the person you want to be this year—the way you'd like to look, a place you'd like to visit, something you'd like to have—cut it out and put it aside. This is something everyone in your house can do. Kids especially love this project, but it's also great to do by yourself.

Go to an art-supply store or five-and-ten and buy poster boards, then go through all the pictures and words you cut out and decide which are the best. Your choices can be artistic, practical, truthful, or fantastic. When you have assembled what really represents the person you are or want to be, start gluing the words and pictures to the poster board in a collage. This is called a Dream Board.

Your Dream Board can have empty space, or the pictures can cover the entire surface. The important thing is that what you paste down is how you see yourself. When you've finished, discuss your Dream Board with your family or friends, tell them what appeals to you about your choices, and then put up your Dream Board so that you'll see it every day.

5 January *Put all the used-up Dream Board scraps and other unwanted magazines in a big pile, and, together with bottles, cans, and newspapers, get them ready for recycling.* If your community has regular recycling, put them out on the appointed day. If you have to take this stuff to a recycling center, do it within a week. If your town does not provide you with the opportunity to recycle, write to your mayor or town council and tell them that recycling should be an integral part of your community's services.

6 January *Incorporate physical exercise as a regular part of your day.* You would never think of not eating, so apply that principle to exercise as well. Pick one or more activities that you like—swimming, running, bicycling, working out, dancing, hiking—and, if you are a beginner, start by doing it twenty minutes per day at least three times a week.

If you can't remember the last time you did any exercise, you'll be surprised at how quickly you can get yourself into shape. If you've been exercising regularly, decide if you need to raise your level or just maintain the pace.

Make sure you warm up and stretch before your workout and cool down and rest afterward. If your climate isn't hospitable in winter, join a gym if finances permit, or work out at home. Put on your favorite music and dance in your living room, or dress properly, with comfortable shoes, and go out for a walk. Exercise has been proven to regulate intake of food, clear the mind, and balance emotions.

Take every opportunity you can to MOVE. Park your car some distance from your destination and walk a few extra blocks. Go to the corner store in the morning to get the newspaper instead of having it delivered. Walk around your neighborhood and notice the changes taking place as one season follows another. Rather than having a meeting in a stuffy office or over a large midday meal, ask your colleague if he or she would like to meet during a brisk stroll. You'll find it easier to stay awake, and much more productive.

7 January *Decide that this year will be your most prosperous to date.* Think about all the things you like to do, all the things that you could spend hours doing, that you would do even if you weren't being paid to do them. Write them down on a sheet of paper and see if your current work situation incorporates any of them.

If you're not working, pretend that your life is your job and do the same thing. Determine if the life you are living is really you, is really what you want to be doing, by listing all the things that please you. If you don't know what makes you happy, think of the times when you most enjoyed your life and try to reconstruct what comprised that enjoyment. This may take some time—days, weeks, or months—but keep it in mind.

If you are doing on a steady, day-to-day basis that which you love to do, acknowledge it right now. Tell yourself how fortunate you are, and express your gratitude for your good choices as often as you can, preferably when you first wake up and when you get into bed at night.

If you find yourself off the track, start thinking about how you can rearrange your job so that you can love it, really love it. Look into delegating tasks that take you away from your true skills and talents. If there's no way you can transform your job so that it pleases you, start thinking about getting another job, or another career for that matter. These changes do not need to be carried out immediately. Start with the thought, the idea, the vision. Actions will follow at the right time. Imagine yourself doing exactly what it is you want to be doing, and seek out people who are already doing it for guidance.

8 January   *Telephone people you've been meaning to talk to and tell them you've been thinking about them.* Wish everyone you can a prosperous, healthy New Year. Go out of your way to be supportive of their resolutions. Encourage their ideas.

Tell them they can accomplish whatever their hearts desire, and that they can call on you whenever their confidence needs boosting. Support for friends and loved ones is a rare and great gift.

Resolve that this is the year you're finally going to do what you've been promising yourself you were going to do each year. Write down in positive statements the things you want to have happen in your life this year. Write them as if they are already real: "I am feeling healthy and fit and weighing 125 pounds; I am getting along splendidly with everybody in my family; I am buying that new watch I've been wanting."

Forgive yourself for not having done these things before. Tell yourself that you did the best you could, and decide that there is no reason why you can't have exactly what you want to have, or be exactly the person you want to be.

9 January   *Make appointments to take care of all the niggling little life things that always end up being put off.* Call the dentist to get your teeth cleaned and examined. Call the auto mechanic and set up an appointment for an oil change, tune up, tire rotation, new brake shoes, etc.

Getting little things done is often a prelude to getting bigger things done. Once you get into the habit of accomplishment, you'll find that the big things don't seem so big. Big jobs, broken down into their component parts, suddenly become a series of little jobs, all of which you can handle.

Building a solid brick wall is a hard job; laying one brick a thousand times is easier.

10 January   *Ask someone to help you do something, regardless of the size of the project.* You might think that the bigger the job, the closer you have to be to the person you ask for help, but that's not always the case. Sometimes people with whom you are in infrequent contact will oblige the most burdensome requests, like helping you move your six-room apartment with a rented truck.

Asking for help is something every happy person knows how to do. It's an art form, and you'll get better and better at it the way you get better at anything—with practice. Don't worry about paying *this person* back. Life offers you many opportunities to reciprocate. Help whomever you can, whenever you can.

Also, when you ask with confidence, expecting your sincere solicitation to be met with a rousing, "Well, of course I'll help you address invitations," your chances of this happening increase tremendously. And if the first several people turn you down, you have two choices: you can keep going until someone finally says yes, or you can do the job yourself. The point of this exercise is to practice asking without shame or timidity, not necessarily to receive—at least not this time.

11 January   *Volunteer to do someone you know a favor.* It doesn't even have to be someone you know

very well. In fact, offering your services to a person you don't know well, but would like to know better, is an ideal way to begin to deepen a friendship.

Think carefully about someone you know who would be delighted if you offered to help him or her with something, who would really appreciate and value your help, and who would thank you sincerely. Go ahead, call her up. Or better yet, show up at her door and say, "Okay, my friend, you got me for the next three hours. What'ya got to do?"

If you turn out to be wrong, and the person you chose ran your derriere ragged and didn't so much as thank you for it, don't feel bad. Simply congratulate yourself for extending your services, and know that your generosity will come back to you some other time.

12 January *Do something completely out of the ordinary, completely out of character for you.* If you've never given a homeless person a dime, give the first one you see today a dollar and tell him to have a nice day. If you're convinced you look terrible in hats, wear one, and act as if it's the most natural thing in the world for you.

Make sure at least one person recognizes that you're a little different today, and try to get as many opinions of the new you as possible. When you go to bed tonight, think back on the most humorous or memorable moment of the day, relive it, and tell yourself that you'll have many more of these moments each time you act out of character.

13 January   *Think about someone you admire.* It doesn't have to be a famous person, and it doesn't
have to be a dead person, although it might be. Think about
why you admire this character, about the qualities he or she
has (or had) to justify your admiration. Is it the way your
best friend handles conflict, or the virtuosity of a famous
cellist?

Find out more about this person. You don't have to know
everything, just something more than you know already. If
it's someone famous, read an article or biography about him
or her. If it's someone with whom you're acquainted, tell him
you'd like to know more about him and ask a question or two.
If this embarrasses you, ask someone else about him.

Think about what it would take to develop the qualities
in yourself that you so admire in this person. Tell yourself it
might not be so difficult, after all, to be as sexy as Sophia
Loren, as powerful as Napoleon, or as kind as Mother
Teresa.

14 January   *Read an old newspaper or magazine.* It doesn't have to be from another century, although if
you want to go back that far there are still many choices.
Something from within the last few years will do.

One undeniable pleasure I derive from waiting in the office of a doctor or dentist is reading old magazines. I can always count on the medical profession to save a few issues from the year before, and I often find myself avidly reading about an event that has already transpired. It's consistently interesting to see how interpretations of occurrences change over time, and even recent events soon take on the look and feel of ancient history—given our event-glutted world.

If you really want to expand on this idea, go to the library and spend a couple of hours reading newspapers and magazines from a different time. You can read the news of the time you were born, when you entered first grade, or when your parents or grandparents were married. You can read your local paper, or familiarize yourself with the national or international scene.

Reading a vintage copy of *The New York Times* or *The Saturday Evening Post* is one of the best ways I know for understanding how different life is today from what it was yesterday. It's a great opportunity to consider what we've lost—and gained—in the interim.

15 January, Martin Luther King, Jr.'s Birthday

Examine a prejudice. It doesn't have to be about race, gender, color, nationality, or sexual preference, but it might be. Maybe you have a thing about lawyers. Well, look at them a little more closely. Try to figure out if all lawyers are as unpalatable as you think.

Ask someone at work if his lawyer is unpretentious, non-competitive, and easy to get along with, the kind of person you want to invite to a baseball game if you're lucky enough to have an extra ticket.

Then try to figure out if your prejudice can withstand the light of scrutiny. Are all children loud and noisy? Does every dog jump up and lick your face when you visit? Are all New Yorkers abrupt? Or are these merely stereotypes that do nothing but prevent us from really examining the source of our prejudice? Is it just too comfortable to maintain the stereotype rather than be obliged to change our opinion?

Better yet, sit down and actually have a conversation with a lawyer—if you can.

16 January   *Be silent for a day.* Find out what life is like without the necessity to respond to everything, to comment, to expend your energy speaking.

Go about your day as if everything else were exactly the same, only do not utter a sound. Pretend you're a medieval monk whose monastic order has sworn you to silence. If you can't do this at work, plan to do it on the weekend. If you must communicate with others, carry a small notebook or blackboard and scribble comments.

How does not speaking affect your mood? What do you sacrifice? What do you gain? What is the trade-off? How much of what you say is merely noise to fill in a perceived vacuum, to ward off feeling things deeply, to hold life at arm's length?

Notice how people respond to you. Do they become hostile? Dismissive? Or are they understanding and supportive of your decision to spend one day abstaining from what you do without hesitation every day?

Watch your energy level. Are you more motivated to act, more aware, or do you find your level of interest faltering without the glue of speech to keep you connected? Do you have more time than usual? Are you more in touch with your feelings and inner life?

17 January *Send someone flowers.* Think about the person you'd like to give them to, and try to imagine what kind of flowers he'd like. Make sure you go to the flower store and pick out the flowers yourself. It's okay to get recommendations from the florist, but make sure the decisions are yours.

After you have left the store, imagine that you grew these flowers yourself, picked them, and are sending your spirit along with them. See the flowers as emissaries of your feeling for the person who is about to receive them. Think about why you have chosen this particular person. Do you want to thank him? Woo him? Make up with him? Surprise him? Startle him? Impress him? Whatever the reason, remember to send the feeling along with the flowers, even if you decide to send them anonymously.

18 January *Start a journal.* You don't have to write every day—you can do it when the mood strikes—but it should be often enough to establish continuity. Two entries a year is too few, while every day may be too demanding. Three to five entries a month is a good number, but more is fine too.

Rather than record every little event that happens in your life, think about what your life means to you as you write. Make sure your entries are dated, and written either in a book devoted to this project, or, if you write on loose sheets or at a computer, bound into some sort of book so that all the writings are together.

Write whatever comes to mind, even if it doesn't make sense or please you. Don't censor yourself. Don't judge your writing for accuracy, grammar, consistency, etc. When something comes up about which you feel strongly, or you have an opinion that you think is worthwhile, rather than express it to someone else, write it in your journal. Before long you'll be in the habit of noting your feelings about your life with ease, and you'll be glad you have a record of them in the future.

19 January   *Spend the day with a child, either your own or someone else's, and see the world through his or her eyes.*

Let the child lead you. Do whatever it is she wants to do, for however long she wants to do it. Have no judgments about her activities. Adopt the same air of importance that a young boy ascribes to collecting rocks and placing them in a paper bag, or that a five-year-old girl gives to pretending she is a ballerina. Pretend along with her.

Do whatever it takes to become a child for the time you spend with him or her. Forget for the moment that you are an adult with cares, concerns, worries, problems, and irritations. Have the ideas come from the child, and enjoy them along with her.

20 January   *Take a long, slow, hot bubble bath.* Make sure you stay in the tub as long as you want to. Don't allow any interruptions to your luxuriating. If you're still in the bathroom after an hour, congratulate yourself on your stamina. Learning to linger is a true art.

21 January *Look at your budget and buy something of very high quality.* Don't scrimp on this one particular item. If you love to read, go out and spend ten dollars on an embroidered bookmark with a beautiful design. If you like to write letters, buy some handsome stationery that makes you feel like royalty when you sit down to write. Consider buying a beautiful new pen as well. If you like to have fresh flowers in your home, buy a vase that does them justice, something that is obviously extravagant, which will represent a gift to yourself in an area of your life that you deeply cherish.

22 January *Listen very carefully to those around you.* Don't take it for granted that you've ever really heard these people before, even if you hear them every day. Imagine that you have suddenly been granted extraordinary powers of hearing.

Listen with your heart as well as your mind and ears. Try to hear the truth behind what the other person is saying, not just the words themselves. Imagine that you can hear between the sentences to what is really going on in the other person's head and listen to his inner voice.

When you are not conversing with anyone, listen to your own inner voice, the part of you that "knows" beyond logic or reason what is real. Hear what you are saying when you are supposedly still, when there is ostensibly nothing going on in your mind. What kind of messages do you get? What do they mean to you? Are you tuned in to your own inner voice, or are you ignoring what is coming through?

23 January   *Go through the entire day without watching or listening to the news or reading the newspaper.* Try your best to shut out the outside world, and concentrate on your own world instead. If someone you encounter wants to talk about current events or the political scene, politely inform him or her that you're taking a short break from things over which you have little control and are focusing on things you can command.

Following the news day after day can induce a feeling of depression and helplessness. Taking a respite from the constant negativity of the world scene can be rejuvenating.

Fill up the time you normally devote to following the news by doing anything else you love to do—talk to a friend, read, listen to music, go for a walk, visit your favorite restaurant—and make sure you take note at the end of the day if you feel different from the way you normally feel.

24 January *Dine by candlelight.* It doesn't matter whether you share a meal with one special person, four aunts and uncles and six kids—or you dine alone. However many join you at your table, light at least two candles, and become aware of how differently everyone relates to one another.

Observe the flickering color on a friend's face, or the way in which your kids become polite at the table, or how Aunt Gladys tells you the story of the last time she ate supper by candlelight. Make sure everyone is aware of how special the evening is, and ask them how often they'd like to do this again.

25 January *Plan your birthday celebration.* If you've already had your birthday, do this activity earlier in the year, before your birthday. Include everyone with whom you'd like to spend the day, and tell them that you want this birthday to be a very special event.

If you'd like, stay home from work and spend time accepting little gifts from the people in your life who are closest to you. Or go to work, having made sure ahead of time that everyone knows it's your birthday and that someone has planned a party in your honor. Actually, it's a good day to be at work, because it's the one day of the year that you'll be regarded with some degree of specialness.

Try something different for this birthday. Instead of being treated by the people who take you out, treat them instead. Invite the people with whom you feel a genuine bond to lunch or dinner, and then pick up the check. You'll astonish your group, and also get treated by them at other times during the year. This is a tradition in other countries. Once, in Italy, we were invited to celebrate the birthday of an old friend. The occasion is still memorable for the exquisite food, the warm feelings, and the sense of wonder and awe I felt when the guest of honor proudly picked up the tab.

26 January   *Join a support group.* It can be a group for couples communication or for people dealing with aging parents or runaway teenagers. It can be a group for eating disorders, drug abuse, or losses in pregnancy.

If you've had personal difficulty and would like to have a network of people around you who have gone or are going through the same, a support group may be just what you require. It will allow you to see that you are not alone, that your pain is shared, that other people can sometimes articulate better than you can what you are thinking and feeling.

If you're embarrassed or uneasy about this, if you don't feel comfortable sharing your pain with strangers, if you are not a "joiner," bear in mind that these groups often deal with these very issues, that the majority of people feel this way at first, and that the people who run support groups are sensitive to your needs. You can always go and listen, without saying anything, until you feel more comfortable there.

27 January *If and when you watch the Super Bowl, enjoy the game to the fullest, but try not to care too much who wins.* Note the level of skill displayed by each team and the individual players. See how expertly or inexpertly they perform their assigned tasks. Watch each play as if it were a step in a very complex but beautiful dance, and try to minimize the competitive, us versus them, good guys and bad guys aspect of the hoopla.

If the team you root for wins, try to figure out if your feeling of elation is genuine, long-lasting, or deep. If your team loses, think of how much pleasure you derived as they got to the Super Bowl. Remember also that they played the entire game without once thinking of you, and that you had no control over the outcome. Living and dying with a team is like being in love with someone who does not know you exist.

If you bet a lot of money on the game, ignore this suggestion and skip to tomorrow.

28 January *Take some form of public transportation.* If you live in or near a big city, take a bus, train, subway, ferry, streetcar, or plane. Leave your car at home. If there is absolutely no way you can get to public transportation, ask a friend to pick you up.

When you're among these fellow passengers, imagine that you have all been placed together for a specific purpose. Speculate as to what it might be. What possible lesson could all these people be teaching you, or might you be teaching them?

Let your imagination take over, and see beyond the immediate and the given. Developing your imagination can expand the possibilities in your life. What creative effort could this particular group of people do well? A choir? Cheerleading squad? Construction crew? Amish village? Assign roles to various people. Try to imagine yourself the director of a movie and this your cast. What kind of movie is it? A romantic comedy? Cops and robbers? A horror movie?

29 January   *Play hooky from work.* Come up with some flimsy excuse and don't go in. Consider this a free day, like when you were a kid and it snowed and, ears glued to the radio, you found out at 7:38 A.M. that your school was closed.

Don't think about work at all; think about everything *but* work. If you have to stay in your house all day because you can't be seen out on the town, laze around and watch soap operas or read a particularly trashy novel. Make yourself a wonderful breakfast, get in touch with a few friends, and pretend you're Ferris Bueller. Who knows—you might enjoy this so much you'll do it a few times a year.

30 January *Give up something you know is not good for you.* If you drink six cups of coffee a day, or smoke too many cigarettes, or drink a lot of beer, go a day without doing any of this and see how it feels. See what life is like without these substances filtering your experience. What does food taste like? How does it feel to carry out a task without the impact of coffee?

Do you want to stop biting your nails, interrupting people, driving too fast? Give it up for one day. Ask everyone around you to reinforce your decision and help you focus your awareness on the behavior you wish to improve. Observe yourself without judgment. Turn this day into a small—but significant—beginning.

31 January *Keep a success log.* Have pen and paper or a small dictaphone with you all day and record every significant thing you did. Success is individual. Decide for yourself what to record. They don't have to be big things. Did you turn down that piece of pie at lunch? Did you make every call you had to at work, or not speak crossly to your kids once? Write it all down.

Watch your list grow as the day progresses. As you hit ten successes, shoot for twenty-five. When you hit twenty-five, go for forty. At the end of the day, read over your list and take note of how much you accomplished. The criteria for accomplishment are yours and yours alone. Something trivial to one person can seem insurmountable to another. See if today's list is unusual or ordinary for you. If you have forty-seven accomplishments and it's a normal day, think for a moment how successfully you manage your life.

Enlarging Your Comfort Zone

The most common mistake people make when trying to create more happiness in their lives is playing it too safe. By confining your range of activities to only those you know will make you happy, either because you've done them before or because they are not unlike what you normally do, you cut yourself off from exploring parts of yourself that you may never know existed, parts that could be developed and are simply waiting to give you pleasure.

Clearly the enemy of happiness is predictability and complacency. Living a life is similar to running a business, and anyone who has ever had a hand in making decisions on a daily basis about which merchandise to buy, which clients to cultivate, which direction to head, knows the terrain. If the business does not grow, at least in some way, it contracts, perhaps not immediately, but certainly before long. There is no healthy business anywhere that is not growing—in vision, in customers or clients, in stores or outlets, and/or in its range of goods and services.

It's exactly the same with happiness. If you rely year after year on the familiar, on the safe, on the same old tired formula, you will find your life providing you with less and less happiness. Life needs to be revitalized, reexamined, tinged with the excitement of the new and different. Whenever I find myself growing restless or stale, I do something that is out of my normal routine. I'll invite an unusual guest to dinner, greet a perfect stranger with a rousing "hello," spend a morning or afternoon in an art museum seeing a new exhibition, or play hooky from work and visit a place I've never been to. Before long, the funk is gone.

If you keep the expansion of your comfort zone as an abiding objective in life, opportunities to derive pleasure from the unfamiliar will present themselves to you.

February

1 February   *Imagine you had only six months to live.* What would you do? What kind of changes would you make? Where would you live? What kinds of things would you surround yourself with?

Live today as if this had actually been told to you, that you had already gotten over the shock of disbelief, and that you are now doing everything with that knowledge. Notice if your life is similar or different from the way you normally live it, if the people who are close to you are those with whom you would like to share your final months.

Be honest but gentle with the people around you. Take the first steps toward making peace with everyone whom you believe has wronged you, or who believes that you have wronged him. If this is too great a task, choose one person. Acknowledge the strain between you. Express your regret that your relations have not been good. Explore ways of making amends. Forgive the past.

How does making peace feel? How comfortable are you with forgiveness, or forgiving? Is it far from your normal response, or close to it?

2 February, Groundhog Day   *Do something nice for an animal.* Play with a dog, stroke a cat, feed pigeons or ducks in a nearby park, or take care of a friend's pet for a day.

Be aware of the animal's life, what his concerns are, how he relates to you, to himself, and his fellow animals and surroundings. What makes him feel good? When does he respond most fully to you?

See who takes the first step toward closeness. Is it you, or the animal? Is he trusting or wary? Does he seem to enjoy your company more than you enjoy his, or vice versa?

Try to determine how the animal makes his decisions, on what basis he acts. If by the end of the day you feel you know a rabbit better than you ever thought possible, recall the feeling of learning about something for the first time, when you discovered, for instance, that some animals hibernate in winter. See if your feelings today are similar.

3 February *Fall asleep reading one of your favorite books, choosing one of your favorite passages.* Make sure that reading this book is the last thing you do today, and read up to the point at which you can no longer keep your eyes open. Then slowly put the book down, turn off the light, and, with a smile on your face, close your eyes.

4 February *Start getting your taxes ready.* Make an appointment to see your accountant, or, if you do

your taxes yourself, pick a date and time at which you will complete the task and mark it on your calendar.

Get all your receipts, check stubs, invoices, and documents together in one place so that when you or your tax person goes through the forms the documentation will be in perfect order and you won't have to think about the drudgery for the next two months.

After the forms are completed, send them in immediately if you are entitled to a refund. If you owe money, wait until April 15 to file.

5 February   *Begin to plan a vacation.* Start thinking about where you would like to go, when, and with whom, and discuss the possibilities with everyone who's interested. Try to reach a consensus before too long and start making inquiries about a trip, whether it's for two days or two weeks.

Think about yourself in this vacation spot, what you'll be doing, eating, seeing, and feeling as you go from day to day. Decide if you'd like to visit a place for the first time or return to a spot of which you have fond memories. Hold in your mind an image of this vacation as you begin to make plans, as you see those plans crystallize, and as the time for your trip draws closer and closer.

Keep brochures or posters of the place you want to visit nearby, so that you can enjoy and dream about the vacation long before you get there.

6 February *Let yourself cry.* It's a great way to release the buildup of accumulated tensions, and it can make you feel tremendously alive to sob quietly or out loud.

Do something that will draw out tears. The best way to do this is to rent a movie that makes you cry. Even though you know the story, or at least the ending, and are prepared for what is going to happen, the movie will probably still make you cry. Ask your local video store what the best tearjerkers are. If they can't recommend one, try *Love Story* or *Terms of Endearment.*

After the movie, get in touch with the feelings engendered by what transpired on the screen. What constitutes the poignancy of human existence? What is the nature of tragedy? Why has the tragic figure been a part of human drama since the beginning of civilization?

Become aware of how much energy is released during your cry, how tired but clear you feel afterward, the depth of your emotions.

If you have unresolved grief, take the opportunity to become aware of it today. See the connection between what you just witnessed and your own tragic history.

7 February *Eat no beef, pork, veal, lamb, fowl, or fish for a day.* See what it feels like to be a vegetarian. For breakfast, give up the bacon, ham, or sausage. At lunch, eat a salad or have a falafel sandwich. At dinnertime, make a vegetable casserole and buy bread that was just baked. Act as if you always eat this way, that eating fruits and vegetables and grains is your normal diet.

There are many nonmeat everyday foods you can make a meal out of—potatoes, rice, bread. Don't think about not getting enough protein. People in many parts of the world eat little or no meat and they do just fine.

Many foreign cuisines use grains and legumes as staples. Try one of them. Middle Easterners prepare chick peas and eggplant; Asians use vegetables and bean curd. Today would be a good day to try a cuisine you've never had before.

8 February   *Complete each task you begin.* Before you allow yourself to move on to anything else, complete what you've already started.

Plan your tasks according to the time you have to complete them. If you only have five minutes before you are required to do something or be somewhere, make sure the project you begin can be completed in five minutes.

After each task, remark to yourself how good it felt to finish something, enjoying the sheer, simple pleasure of deciding to do something and then doing it. As the day wears on, you might want to increase the length or complexity of your tasks. By early evening, you'll be completely immersed in whatever you're doing. Even if you feel exhausted, it will have been worth the effort.

9 February *Completely serve another person.* Choose someone you really like and devote the entire day to catering to his or her every whim, regardless of its difficulty or ease. No task is too large or too small, too complex or too simple.

While you're doing this, examine what it's like to be completely devoted to another person, to dissolve your own requirements and become totally dedicated to someone else's. How does it make you feel? Do you resent it? Is it easier than you expected? Are you able to carry out these tasks at the same time as you maintain your self-respect, or do you feel used and abused?

10 February *Ask someone to be completely devoted to you.* It could be the same person you served yesterday, but it doesn't have to be. What's important is the feeling of being served, regardless of who is doing the serving.

See if you can lead someone gently and respectfully, without losing your integrity or compromising the dignity of your server. What is it like to feel completely supported, to have unwavering loyalty, to be the object of devotion? Is it something with which you're comfortable, or do you feel undeserving of this level of attention?

Talk about the experience with the person who served you. If it was the person you were with yesterday, compare experiences. What was more comfortable for you? Server or served? What about your partner?

11 February *Give yourself more time to do things.* Whether you're working on a project, in transit, or just killing time until the next event begins, add extra minutes or hours to the amount of time you think it will take and slow down your speed to use that extra time.

If it normally takes you twenty minutes to drive to work, allow thirty. Experience the pleasure of taking your time, of knowing that you are not feeling rushed. If you can whip up a meal in fifteen minutes, take forty-five. Become aware of how you feel doing the task with the extra period built in. Does the passage of time seem slower or sped up? Are you adding to the enjoyment of these routine tasks, or is your equilibrium thrown off? Do you feel indulged, graced, luxuriated?

Is there much extra time in your day? If so, do you enjoy it, or does it make you feel anxious? What is it like not to be rushed? Is that something you'd like to feel more often?

12 February, Lincoln's Birthday

Do something to improve your knowledge of history. It doesn't have to be American history, but it's appropriate to focus on that. Rent a movie about the Civil War, like *Glory.* Read an article, or begin reading a historical novel or history book, Gore Vidal's *Lincoln,* for example. Make sure you know one more fact, understand a past time a little better, than you did this morning.

One way to move up the history learning curve is to focus on a time about which you know almost nothing and learn as much as you can in as short a period as you can. Every era has its charms and peculiarities and can illuminate the human condition.

13 February   *Between the time you wake up and the time you get out of bed, completely plan your day.* As you lie awake, go over in your mind the clothes you're going to wear, what you're going to accomplish, whom you're going to see, when these events are scheduled to take place, and the importance of each. Imagine that you're going to have enough time to do everything and will feel totally at ease throughout the day.

When you feel comfortable with your plans, get out of bed and tell yourself that you're going to have the most productive day of your life.

14 February, Valentine's Day

Immerse yourself in love and romance. Devote the entire day to thoughts, activities, and people that bring out the romantic part of you, with whom you can be your most romantic self.

Read books and stories about love, and pretend that you've just met your husband, wife, or partner, and are still courting, still trying to impress him or her with your timing and fine sense of wooing.

Have love on your mind constantly. Think of things that will make you sexier, more alluring, more compelling, more attractive. Use candy, flowers, clothing, massage, or sweet nothings as your props. Have dinner in bed with your lover. Light candles and build a fire. Exude a sense of romance, of 1001 languid Arabian Nights. Exchange sexual fantasies. Play music that puts you and your partner in the mood for you-know-what.

If you're unattached, imagine yourself spending the day with your true partner. What would you do? Where would you go? Do these things and go to these places alone and imagine your partner is there with you, sharing these romantic moments. Who knows—he or she may be waiting for you just around the corner.

15 February *Put everything you value most—the objects (regardless of their monetary value) whose loss would upset you—in one place.* If there are large things as well as small ones, separate them according to size.

Be ruthless in choosing what to include. It doesn't matter how often you use these things, or whether you use them at all: your first bracelet, a ticket for the Paris *métro* from a trip twenty years ago, your Mickey Mouse Club ears. What matters is that you want to know where these treasured possessions are at all times, and don't want to search half the drawers and rooms of your house when you want to look at them, or hold them, or use them to remind you of a certain time, significant person, or important event in your life.

Look at these items whenever you feel the need to connect with your past, to conjure up the feeling of a different time in your life, to feel sentimental. Rainy days are especially suited to this.

16 February *Put on a movie marathon.* Rent at least two indisputably hilarious movies, invite a bunch of friends—the more the merrier—to your home, make popcorn, and laugh your head off.

17 February   *Visit a town close by that you've never been to before.* Go there as if you've just landed in a foreign country and see the place with fresh eyes. Find out what there is to do, to see, where the best place to eat is, or what the history of the town or city is.

Walk down the main street and look at the windows of the stores. Is this place like the neighborhood in which you live? What's the feel of the terrain? Friendly and inviting, or cold and unwelcoming? Could you imagine yourself living here? Is it the kind of place you'd like to return to, or is one visit enough?

18 February   *Fix up something you've used frequently over the years.* Perhaps you have a chair that could use refinishing, or a copper teakettle badly in need of polish. Do you have a map you've used so often that it needs to be taped and refolded? It could be as simple as that.

Remember how it felt when you first started using it, how special, shiny, and unmarked it was. Try your best to get as close to its original condition as possible. Put on that extra coat of paint or polish, or get the highest quality replacement part you can find. As you perform this project, take note of how much pleasure this item has provided you, and genuinely demonstrate your honor and respect for it by doing the best job you can.

19 February *Ask someone you admire to lunch.* Your reasons for admiring this individual can be trivial or serious. You may be the only person you know who admires him or her, and the source of your admiration may be obscure—even incomprehensible—to everyone else. That's not important. What matters is that *you* admire this person.

When you're having lunch with the recipient of your admiration, let the person know how you feel about her and why. She may have no idea you feel this way, nor have ever felt herself worthy of admiration. By informing her of your feelings, you reinforce the qualities in her you find admirable, and also strengthen your own capacity for these same qualities by affirming your admiration of them. The more you talk about and suffuse yourself with these qualities, the more you draw them to you.

20 February *Do everything for positive reasons, not negative ones.* If you have an obligation to fulfill, instead of thinking that someone will be irritated with you if you don't do it, think of how good it will feel to fulfill this

responsibility, or better yet, of why you incurred this obligation to begin with.

Rather than brushing and flossing your teeth because they will rot and fall out if you don't, think of how wonderful it feels to have a clean, healthy mouth. Rather than adhering to the speed limit because you're afraid of getting pulled over and cited by the police, think of how much safer it is to drive lawfully, how much more responsible to the environment. Complete your school assignments not because you fear humiliation by your teacher, but because in doing so you learn so much more, and also practice carrying out assigned tasks.

Over time, doing things for positive reasons creates positive responses in your life. Doing things for negative reasons creates negative ones.

21 February *Pay attention to everything you eat and drink.* What you put into your body becomes you, so think about the connection between how much and what you're eating and drinking, and your health, well-being, state of mind, and ability to take charge of your life. Too much food with too little nutritional value can have a negative effect on your mood and attitude, as well as your body.

Eat or drink only what you find delicious. Eat slowly, carefully chewing every mouthful, and when you feel full, STOP! Forget about the starving masses in India and China;

cleaning your plate long after you've had enough is not going to feed them. Eat only in designated eating areas—like the kitchen or dining room—sitting down. Make each meal a special part of your day and avoid eating in between. Create an atmosphere of calm, with no distractions. TV, chaos, and arguments don't mix well with food. Wait until it is quiet and peaceful before you begin a meal.

Regardless of how close to or far from your ideal weight you feel you are, accept yourself. Look at yourself in a mirror. Say out loud that you accept and love yourself, that any change you want to make to your body will make you all the more beautiful or handsome, and that it is becoming easier and easier to realize your ideal shape.

22 February, Washington's Birthday

Learn one new fact about the way the United States got started, or about George Washington. What were the events that led to the break with England? How did Washington get to be appointed commander in chief of the Revolutionary Army, and then get elected president? Who voted for him? Who ran against him?

How did the Declaration of Independence get written? When did the Liberty Bell crack? Why did almost every European country fight alongside the colonies against England? Where did Benedict Arnold commit treason against the United States? Did he ever confess his guilt?

23 February   *Visit a public library.* Make sure you give yourself enough time to get into the feeling of being among all those books, any of which you can pull off the shelf and imbibe for as long as you'd like.

You can take ten books and go through each of them quickly, or sit down with one and start reading from the first page. You can stroll down a dozen aisles and marvel at the wealth of information on a multitude of subjects, or stay in one place and note the wealth of information available on each subject.

Read a magazine. Peruse the videotape library. Ask the librarian to help you find a certain book. Be aware of the infinite variety of passions that have been expressed through the written word, and that you can avail yourself of the breadth and depth of them anytime you want.

24 February   *Search for something you've lost or misplaced, but not when you need it.* Carefully look through everything that could be blocking this article from view. Make sure you give yourself enough time to do the job properly.

Think about where and when you last saw the item. Ask anyone who might know its whereabouts if he's seen it.

Come up with some hunches, even if they're long shots, and follow up on them.

Pretend you're eight years old and you're on a treasure hunt. Open every drawer, look in every closet, go through every file. Be open to finding it in a place you least expect. Take a moment or two to linger on things you do come across that bring back memories, which you realize you can use in your life right now, which remind you of plans you once had on which you never followed up.

If you find the original item, reflect upon it for a moment or two before putting it where you know you won't misplace it. If you don't find it, stop searching only when you have assured yourself that there are no other places you could look.

25 February   *Take a roll of pictures of one person or thing.* It doesn't matter if the film is black and white or color, slides or prints, just choose one object and photograph it. It could be your boyfriend, your daughter, your cat, your favorite chair, a flower, or the Sunday paper.

Make sure no two photographs are the same. Shoot from every conceivable angle. Stand above it, under it, to the side. Shine a light on it. Put it on the windowsill. If you're using a single-lens reflex camera, use different light exposures. Stand close; stand far away.

When the pictures come back, notice how different the object appears in each shot, how something looks one way from one angle and different from another. Sometimes the differences are subtle, sometimes profound. See that something looks the way it does only from your standpoint relative to the object. Which one is the truest representation? Or are they all true?

26 February *Make a list of the things you want to do today and cross off each one as you complete it.* The longer the list the better. The more tasks you can think of early, the more accomplished you will feel at the end of the day when you have completed most or all of them.

Watch the horizontal lines increase as the day wears on. Do each task in order and see the lines move farther and farther down the list, or do them randomly and see yourself crossing something off here, something off there.

If you do this more than once, keep the lists in a file folder, and the next time you are berating yourself for your laziness or your inability to get things done, pull out the folder and look at all the days on which you succeeded in accomplishing dozens of tasks.

27 February *Write out your life goals.* Allowing enough time so that you won't feel hurried, think about where you are right now and where you'd like to be in the future. Don't panic if nothing comes to you at first, or if

you're not sure that where you think you want to be is really where you want to be. Just go quietly inside yourself, consider what really turns you on, and let ideas that incorporate these qualities come to you.

Then start writing. Where do you want to be a year from now? Five years from now? Ten years from now? What would you like to be doing? With whom would you like to be spending more time? Less time? Are there new people you'd like to bring into your life? Sometimes it's easier to start out in the future and work backward to the present.

Now take a file card and write down your immediate life goal. State it positively, not negatively. "I am meeting my financial obligations with ease," rather than "I don't worry about money anymore." Or, "I am living in Tuscany as a writer of children's books, eating pasta and drinking homemade wine every day with my true partner." Look at this card frequently and say aloud what you've written at least twice a day. Every time you do so you bring yourself closer to your goal.

28 February   *Celebrate something small in a big way.* Did your five-year-old son lose his first tooth? Did a report you worked on lovingly get rave reviews from your boss? Did you finally clean up the yard? Celebrate. Now's the time.

Do something special. Go out for dinner to your favorite restaurant. Invite people with whom you'd like to share your joy and let them know what you're celebrating. Dress up and pull out all the stops. It doesn't have to be your birthday, your kid's birthday, your anniversary, or the Fourth of July to make a big deal about it.

Draw out the idea and think of something every day that you could celebrate in this manner. (It doesn't mean you have to do it. It just means you *could* do it.)

If you make a habit of doing this, the smallest events in your life take on greater significance and confer upon you greater pleasure.

29 February, Sadie Hawkins Day

If you're an unmarried woman, teasingly ask someone to marry you. If you're a man, keep your fingers crossed. If you're already married, this is a free day. You're on your own.

Intention Is
Everything

What do I mean by intention, and why is it everything? People spend much too much time evaluating their actions, and much too little examining their motives. The desire to do everything perfectly (which has a place in life but has gotten out of control lately) is too focused on the end product of an action or activity, rather than on the *initial* motivation. If you feel the need to perfect something, perfect your motives.

Intention is the first step of a happy life and is the source from which all subsequent action springs. If you can purify your motives, if you can refine your intention so that you feel, in your heart of hearts, that what you are doing, or intending to do, or just did, comes out of love rather than fear or selfish interest, then you don't *ever*—need to worry about the effects of your actions. Regardless of how things "turn out," they will always turn out well because they came from your truth, from your honest, best attempt to act upon your intention. Whenever something is not quite working for me, I look at my underlying motives and almost always see the flaw; on the other hand, when my actions are mindfully consistent with who I am, things flow smoothly. When my behavior arises from generosity, caring for the other, learning more about myself, and mutual benefit, I welcome any and all outcomes.

This is really all you need to know about creating happiness. Your actions will almost appear to be guided, and you will attract people and create situations that are meant to assist you if you keep your intention firm, focused, and pure.

March

1 March   *Write a letter to someone special.* The letter doesn't have to be long. Go for quality, not quantity. Think of someone with whom you'd really like to have a conversation and put all the things you would ask or say in words.

Set aside enough time so that you don't feel pressured. An hour would probably do. Get out the writing paper and your favorite pen and sit quietly for a few minutes, or begin to think about what you want to say before you sit down. Then start by imagining that the person is right next to you. It could be someone close to you, or someone in the public eye. What would you like her to know first?

Once you start to write, the rest will come easily. If you momentarily run out of things to say, stop and let your mind wander. Eventually you will come back to the things you want to include in the letter.

When you're finished, mail the letter as soon as possible.

2 March   *Create a photo album of your life.* Go through all your pictures and pick out the ones that are particularly representative, significant, or sentimental. Choose the photos that illuminate a particular time or place. Who were you with? What were you doing? What vacations were special?

You can select one photo for each year, or five per year, or one for every five years. The choice is yours. The important thing is that they all contribute to the story that is your life.

Then get as many photo albums as you need and do your best to put the pictures in chronologically. It doesn't really matter if a June photo turns out to be ahead of a May photo of the same year, or even if the years are a little out of order. You also might want to write dates on pages as a guide. If this project seems overwhelming, spread it out over a period of time. It doesn't have to be completed in one day.

When you assemble your album, look through the photos and see how your life has changed over the years. Try to discern patterns and trends from the people with whom and situations in which you've found yourself. Keep your album up to date.

3 March *Let go of something or someone who has been a chronic irritation.* It doesn't matter if you are sure you're right, or that you can't understand how a misunderstanding could have taken place, or that your former best friend won't talk to you anymore. Do whatever you must to erase the problem, be it reconciling or cutting loose, whichever is appropriate.

This might mean writing a letter, making a phone call, throwing something away, giving a small gift, making a decision, telling someone exactly how you feel—whatever you have to do to put the matter to rest.

It's also not important if the problem is ten years old, or even thirty years old, and you can't confront the person anymore. His or her presence is not crucial. Your action is the key. Just decide that you no longer define yourself by this matter. It is no longer a part of your life. It is no longer an issue. You have officially left it behind.

4 March *Perform a routine out of normal sequence or location.* If you always wash your hair at the end of your shower, do it at the beginning. If you always wake up at 6:30 A.M., wake up earlier or later and adjust your schedule accordingly.

Sleep on the other side of the bed, or, better yet, put your head where your feet normally go. Or move your bed around to face a different direction.

Do other things seem different when you vary your habits ever so slightly? Even the smallest departure from the norm can give you a completely different perspective on life if you pay attention to the particular way you do things. Your awareness of these things, your focus on them, can make you more acutely conscious of larger life choices.

Do you let the dog out before waking up the kids, or after? Who leaves the house first, you or your spouse? Do you drink your coffee at home or at work? Whatever your normal pattern of behavior, change it. If it feels funny, but you have the sense that you might get used to it, try it again sometime.

5 March *Observe yourself without judgment.*
Rather than commenting upon, editorializing about, or evaluating what you do, say, think, and react to, just go through the day without saying to yourself, either silently or out loud, that what you did was good, bad, right, wrong, smart, stupid, too soon, too late, or too anything. Extend this practice to others as well.

Watch yourself doing or saying things with detachment, almost as if someone else is doing or saying them. Pretend the part of you that evaluates your every move is off on vacation, and you don't know when he or she will return. Let yourself move through the day observing your behaviors and thoughts rather than identifying with them.

Be a witness to your own life. Rather than feeling guilty or angry with yourself for being impatient with your kids, witness the interaction as if from the sidelines. Does this feel liberating? After a while, can you see yourself more clearly than before?

6 March *Open a new savings account for a special purchase.* Make sure that your account is devoted entirely to this purpose, whether it's a new car, a trip to Hawaii, a new suit or dress, a bicycle, or a basketball.

Resolve to save the money to do or buy this as quickly as possible.

Put yourself on a regular weekly or monthly schedule in order to increase the amount you save. Even if you can contribute only five dollars per month to the account, make sure your five dollars goes in regularly. If you have extra money left over at the end of a month, deposit that as well.

Tell as many people as you feel comfortable that you're saving for a sapphire ring, or an exercise machine for your home, or the latest CD, and think about how you're going to wear, use, or enjoy this item once you have it. If your purchase is a trek through Nepal, talk to travel agents, look at pictures, and imagine yourself already there as often as you can.

7 March   *Plant fresh herbs, like basil, rosemary, sage, oregano, or parsley.* Think about the herbs with which you most enjoy cooking and find a place to grow them. If you have a yard, a small patch of it will do. If you live in an apartment, plant the herbs in pots.

Find out which plants do well in your area. Seedlings are easier to grow, but if you're feeling ambitious, start by planting seeds.

Growing your own herbs is especially fun for kids, who learn to see the process of growth. It can be a revelation for them to realize that fresh food tastes better, and that herbs don't start out in bottles.

8 March *Do something special with* someone
else's *child.* It could be your niece or nephew, or a neighbor's
or friend's child. Just make sure the small boy or girl is not
your own, and that it's only one child.

Go to a museum, or walk around town and buy her something small but special. Treat her as though she was a little
princess, and talk to her about your life as if she were a good
friend of yours. If you open up to this child, she will start asking you questions as if you were the most knowledgeable person on earth.

Spend enough time together so that you really get to
know one another. Share with her your favorite places to
visit, the TV shows you like best, and what you liked to do
most when you were her age. Try to convey the sense that
deep down you are just like she is, wanting to play and have
fun most of the time. End the day with an ice cream cone, or
whatever food she enjoys.

9 March *Make a list of what you like about*
yourself. The qualities can be trivial or big. You can say that
you are always willing to help a friend, or that you like the
way a wave of hair falls on your forehead. What's important

is that you think about yourself deeply and thoroughly, perhaps in a way you never thought of yourself before.

Be honest. Include only those things that really please you. Are you efficient and responsible about home and car repairs? Do you have a special artistic flair when it comes to your clothes? Is your house always a hospitable haven for your friends and neighbors?

Don't underestimate yourself. Don't overlook or minimize anything. Do you like the sound of your voice? That you're a good listener? That you have a green thumb? That you have leadership qualities that emerge in subtle ways?

Keep your list up to date. Add to it when new things come up, or as you realize that you have more attractive qualities than you first thought.

10 March *Sit back-to-back with someone and express yourselves.* Put aside about a half hour and make a pact with your partner that each of you can talk for fifteen minutes without interruption about anything that's on your mind. What you talk about doesn't necessarily have to pertain to your partner; you may want the opportunity to talk about your inner life, and only want someone to listen.

Often our ability to communicate is affected or even stifled by the unconscious body language of the other person. A furrowed brow, a down-turned mouth, or crossed arms can quickly put a damper on our ability to express ourselves. Sitting back-to-back, and knowing that you have fifteen minutes to talk without interruption, will permit you to open up fully and deeply.

If this activity brings up feelings of discomfort, try to stay with it anyway. In time the discomfort will pass, and you'll appreciate your newly acquired ability to express things you might not have divulged before.

11 March *Immerse yourself in color.* Buy some acrylic paint—with red, blue, yellow, white, and black you can create any color—and make a composition with the most vibrant colors you can imagine.

Put your painting on good quality paper or a canvas from an art supply store. Don't think about what you are going to paint, just think about the colors or color combinations. Ask yourself, "How can I create the most colorful composition?" Mix the tubes until you get the colors that fit your mood, and apply them liberally.

Notice what these colors look like, feel like, and what kind of reaction they induce in you. Do they remind you of something—a past experience or dream, perhaps? Are you surprised at the colors you have chosen for your painting? As you work, don't think about the finished product; rather, go with whatever idea or movement appeals to you from moment to moment. When you like what you have created, stop. When you think your work of art is finished, it probably is.

12 March *Volunteer your time.* There are an infinite number of organizations or services that would love to have you spend a few hours helping them, so pick one and pay a visit.

Think of what you would like to do to help the organization and feel good about yourself at the same time. Is it sitting with a few elderly people and listening to them tell you about their lives? Delivering supplies for a homeless shelter in your community? Or answering the phone for a local fundraising project? At any given moment, a project that you would like to see become more effective could use your help. If you only have an hour to give, then give an hour. If you can devote some time on a regular basis, your cause would find that most welcome.

When you volunteer, think about how much pleasure you are deriving from your efforts and how much they are appreciated. Volunteer at the same place, or spread your time around many causes, whichever feels right.

13 March *Have a lively conversation with someone.* Think about what it means to practice the art of conversation. Make sure your listening skills are as polished as your talking skills, or, if you're someone for whom opening up does not come easily, take this opportunity to practice sharing your thoughts and feelings.

The setting and the partner(s) are crucial. You must feel comfortable where you are. It can be a café, a bar, a restaurant, a park, your office, or, in special cases, your bedroom. To get the conversation going, just start talking about what's on your mind, and say it in a way that invites response or feedback. No monologues. No soliloquies. It's fine to ramble, but make sure you get clearance from the participants before you plunge ahead.

The object of the discussion is the discussion itself. You don't need to solve the world's problems, or even your own. You only need to open up your head and your heart, to listen well, to share your opinions, and to be as honest as you are capable of being. The conversation will flow naturally out of your and your partner(s)' ability to both listen and respond.

14 March   *Look for coincidences.* Pretend that nothing in your life happens at random, that everything takes place according to some plan, even if it has not been revealed to you. Notice every stranger you meet today and see if you run into one of them more than once, or if you encounter something shortly after you were thinking about it.

Become aware of the connections between seemingly unconnected things. Spend the entire day expecting coincidences to happen, awaiting them, believing that coincidences are the way things are supposed to be, and see how many occur. Did you gaze intently at an ad for pecan pie only to go to a friend's house for dinner and find pecan pie for dessert? Were you and someone else the last two people to get in an elevator, only to end up behind her when you bought your lunch, three blocks away?

Tell someone about all the coincidences that happened to you today and see what his reaction is. Try to discover whether people generally believe in coincidence or whether they dismiss the entire notion as poppycock. Regardless of what people think, however, the more you believe in coincidences, the more they will happen.

15 March   *Dress differently.* Whatever your normal attire is, change it. You can dress up or dress down; that's not important. What is important is that in a situation that calls for conformity, you look different from the way you normally look. If you always wear a suit and you absolutely cannot go to the office in overalls, wear a sport jacket, or, if it is out of the question to deviate from your dress code, put on a bow tie, or wear flats instead of heels.

Even the smallest change in attire is significant. If you always wear a belt, try suspenders. If you fix cars, wear a blue bandana around your neck. Change your earrings, the color of your hose, the shade of your lipstick. Be prepared to explain to everyone you meet what prompted you to change your look, and offer a different reason to everyone who asks you.

Do you feel a pulse of excitement as you make these changes? Does the world seem different to you? Are other changes possible? Do small changes give you the confidence to make bigger ones?

Be willing to play the fool. Changes in your life take place when you take risks, and that includes the risk of looking foolish.

16 March *Trade roles with someone.* The person could be your wife, husband, parent, child, co-worker, boss, friend, or, for the truly creative, a relative stranger. For one day, do all the things that person does every day and invite him to do all the things you normally do.

If your wife always cooks dinner and cleans up while you read *The Wall Street Journal,* cook and clean up while she reads *The Wall Street Journal.* Ask your assistant or colleague what she routinely does and do it for her today, at the same time as she does your job.

Do your partner's job as best you can. Proceed with your own innate knowledge and intuition. Get the basic information early, and don't ask too many questions about where things go, what time you put the baby down for a nap, or who handles the car pool throughout the day. Assume that you are on your own and have to get by with whatever information you already have.

As you find yourself being someone else, do you feel energized, or enervated? Is it much more difficult to be a child than you thought, or would you gladly trade places with your eight-year-old? Is your replacement doing your job the way you do it, or is he coming up with different, more creative ways of doing things? What can you learn from seeing your own role performed in a new way?

17 March, St. Patrick's Day

Give someone a gift. It doesn't have to be an expensive gift; something modest will do. But it has to be for someone you've been thinking about, with whom you want to connect, and who would be delighted to receive a gift from you.

You can either give this gift in person or send it in the mail. It can be delivered by a messenger or left at your recipient's doorstep. The gift should be an unmistakable symbol of your relationship, your friendship, the extent of your intimacy, of the moments or memories or dreams you have shared or currently share. It should signify without doubt the quality of who you are and what you mean to each other.

You can acknowledge the help a friend has given you over the years by paying for a professional massage, or let your spouse know how much she means to you by framing a photograph of the two of you.

If the person you have in mind is Irish, make sure there's something green in the package, or take her out for an Irish coffee.

18 March   *Organize a wine tasting.* Invite people to join in, to participate in an exercise in taste. The wines you choose can be the modest table variety, or from a particular grape. This is fun regardless of the level of knowledge of the participants.

You can choose wines from the same category, like Chiantis or merlots or chardonnays, or mix them without regard to type. You might also want to have a tasting that includes both domestic and imported wines. Have some bread and cheese on hand to complement the libations, and supply a pitcher or pot to everyone to pour out the wine that's already been sufficiently tasted. (If you drink all the wine each time you taste, after a while it will all taste the same.)

Place the wines in paper bags and number them. As each wine is tasted, ask the people assembled to write down their impressions. It makes sense to discuss wine words ahead of time, like nutty, fruity, oaky, and young, and have them roll off your tongue. You can even make jokes about them.

See if there is any correlation between the pleasing flavor of a wine and its price. Ask everyone to write a description of his favorite, and award a small prize to the most enticing entry.

19 March   *Write down your dreams.* Immediately after you awake, jot down as much of what you dreamed as you can remember. Try to note details, as insignificant as they appear to be. What was the color of the chair that mysteriously appeared in the living room of the house in which you grew up? What exactly did Joan of Arc say to you when she appeared in the room as you conducted your regular Monday morning staff meeting? Details are important.

When you try to remember your dreams, think about the feelings you had during the night. Were you frightened, elated, confident, angry? Sometimes focusing on the feelings of the dream helps you to remember the details.

If you decide to record your dreams on a regular basis, keep a dream journal. Don't worry about what your dreams "mean." The more you remember, the more you record, the more your dreams will be comprehensible to you. As you take note of them, they will become more vivid, more real. You will soon see how your dreams are a window into your inner life, which is active and wise, and has a lot to teach you.

Keep your dream journal by your bed so that the first thing you do each morning is record last night's dreams. Or get a small dictaphone and put them on tape.

20 March *Take a long walk, away from streets and stores and traffic signals.* Spend at least two hours among trees, grass, water, animals. Spend one hour walking farther and farther from civilization, then walk back to your original point. Or walk in a circular path.

Take your time. See what nature looks like. How do the trees appear to you? Is there a pattern, or do they grow seemingly at random? Do you hear birds singing? Is their chirping the same song each time? Do they seem to respond to one another?

What does the air feel like, look like, smell like? Does it feel the same as the air you normally breathe, or is it different? How so? Is it lighter or heavier, thicker or thinner, clearer or murkier? What sounds do you hear? Does the stillness disturb or soothe you? Are there flowers in your path? Do they move to welcome and embrace you?

Leave everything as you find it. "Take only pictures, leave only footprints."

21 March *Clean out your clothes closets.* Go through every article of clothing and decide if you want to keep or get rid of it. If you can't imagine making these decisions on your own, invite someone whose opinions you trust to be your clothes counselor and executioner.

Be ruthless. If you haven't worn something in a year, chances are you won't wear it in the next year. Get rid of it. Keep only those clothes you really like, the ones you wear a lot. If you see something that might be part of a retrospective on dress in the sixties, it's probably time you donated it to a museum. Getting rid of clothes you have no use for makes room for new clothes to fit comfortably in your closets and wardrobe.

Donate the things you don't want to Goodwill or the Salvation Army, or offer the clothes to your friends or relatives. After you're done you'll feel lighter, airier, and chances are you'll never miss a single item.

22 March   *Plant a tree to remember someone dear to you.* If you have a backyard, that's the ideal place for it. If not, use your imagination to think of an appropriate spot for the tree's permanent home.

You might want to have a little ceremony to honor this person. It doesn't have to be someone who recently passed on, just someone who is significant to you. It could be in honor of your cat or dog, or an important relationship that is over. Make sure you can visit the tree often, and that it's in a safe place.

Every time you look at the tree, think of the person in whose honor the tree was planted. What did he or she mean to you? What did he give you, teach you? Was she a role model, an inspiration, a mentor, a good friend? Was he someone who left suddenly? Speak to the tree as if you were speaking directly to the person and he or she could hear you.

23 March *Don't wear a watch.* Spend the whole day not being able to know what time it is every time you feel the urge.

Don't change your schedule. Conduct this day in the same manner that you live every other day. Make appointments, carry out projects, talk to people on the telephone, run errands. See if you can estimate how much time you are spending on each task. If you absolutely need to know the time, ask someone, but do so only when you have no idea what time it is and it is imperative that you not be late.

What does it feel like not to be bound to time every minute of the day? Does it change the way you go about doing things? Are you more aware of your actions, how long you are taking, or less aware? Does it feel liberating to be without a watch, or frightening? Does time go by faster, or more slowly?

See if your watch is a necessity in your daily life, or just a burden. See if you can be without one more often.

24 March *Play the date game.* Ask someone whose life you'd like to know more about and with whom

you'd like to share more of yourself to join you. Then pick a date in the past, say, January 1979, or September 1983, or, if you go back a bit further than that, June 1957.

Each of you then tells the other what was going on in your life during that month. Where were you working? With whom were you involved? Were you happy or were things not going well? What was the feeling of that time? Were you in transition? Did you just meet someone who was to become significant in your life? If you can't remember that particular month, recount something that occurred shortly before or after.

Keep going for as long as you want. Each of you picks a date and then you start talking. You'll find it's a great way to get to know someone. You can also ask each other questions about that time if you feel you want to know more. If you can't remember exactly, then approximate. Ready? July 1977 . . .

25 March *Imagine your life has just begun.* This is the very first day you are seeing the world. What does it look like to you? What things astound you, amaze you, make you feel good? What about the other side? What things make you fearful, wary, hesitant? To what are you instinctively drawn? What repels you?

Go through the day as if you've never done it before. You've just arrived on Earth from another planet where you were pure spirit, and now you have a body to transport and senses to interpret data. What things turn you on? Where do you want to linger? With whom do you want to spend time?

Do you want to be alone more? Or does a crowded room excite you?

See how much of life the people with whom you come into contact take for granted. Notice other people's reactions to things, whether they listen carefully, if their eyes are fully open. See how much gets by without so much as a notice.

26 March *Listen to the songs you loved as a teen.* Immerse yourself in the music. Play it in the car, at home, and on a little tape recorder at work, if that's feasible. Hearing the music of your teenage years, your mind should believe that it's 1965, or 1981, or 1942.

With each song, think about what you were doing when you first heard it, if you can. If not, think about the time in general. Why did you like this particular music? Did you dance to it? Sing along with it? Listen to it on records, on the radio, or hear it at live concerts? Were you Diana Ross and your sisters the Supremes? Who was your favorite—the Beatles or the Rolling Stones? Or was it the Dave Clark Five?

Do you still like this music? Is it evocative of the time in which you first heard it, or are the memories faint? Is there anyone with whom you can share your pleasure? If so, invite him or her to listen to the tunes with you. Ask him to bring his own favorites and plan a music marathon. If you can, make tapes, and do this as often as the mood strikes.

27 March   *Compliment everyone with whom you interact.* Look for at least one thing associated with each person—friends, family members, co-workers, people who work in stores—about which you can pay an honest compliment.

Make sure the person understands fully that you are paying him or her a compliment. Don't mutter under your breath that the salesperson in the bookstore has an absolutely terrific smile, or merely allude to the fact that your boss has a new tie that's smashing. Come right out with it. "You know, I haven't seen a smile as great as yours in months." Or, "Say, Bob, that's a great new tie you're wearing. It goes perfectly with that shirt you've got on."

There are an infinite number of characteristics that merit positive attention. Looks, manners, attire, consideration, helpfulness, articulateness are but a few. Watch how people light up when you pay them a compliment. But make sure it's honest. If a 300-pound guy comes to deliver your bottled water, you can't say how thin he is. But you can tell him how much you appreciate how carefully he backed up his truck, or that he set the bottle down on the porch without waking the baby.

Complimenting people is a habit, just like any other. And it's one that becomes contagious. People feel great when they receive compliments, and you'll feel great when you give them as well.

28 March   *Pamper your body.* Do something, anything, that makes your body feel good. Get a facial, a massage, a manicure or pedicure. Sit in a hot tub, a Jacuzzi, or mineral springs. Take a stretching class and focus on your muscles, tendons, and ligaments.

Make sure what you do is nurturing, not strenuous at all. The point is to feel the pleasure your body can provide you without stress or pain or endurance. Everything should be geared toward an easy release of the tensions that inevitably build up every day.

See if you can let go of any trepidation and really get in touch with the pleasure your body wants to provide you. Explore different ways that your body can make you feel good, especially ones about which you've been skeptical.

29 March   *Bargain for something.* Regardless of the store, the item or service, don't accept the stated or published price as final. See if you can obtain the item for less money.

Be fair. Don't ruin your chances of success by being unreasonable or insulting. Bargain in good faith, but also keep in mind that prices are not fixed, regardless of what the tag says. Remember, bargaining is a regular feature of other cultures. In fact, it is considered insulting in some cultures not to bargain.

Tell the merchant or salesperson that you really love the item, but that it is a little dear for your pocketbook. Ask if he or she would be willing to sell it to you for $7.50 instead of $12. There is always a reason why it could be sold for less— end of the season, beginning of the season, first sale of the day (a staple of Arab cultures), damage, close-out, whatever.

The merchant will usually level with you and tell you what his lowest price is. If you really want to play hardball and get your price, be prepared to walk out of the store— without hostility—in order to convince your negotiating partner of your seriousness.

See the bargaining process as a game, a test of skill, nerves, and the extent of your tenacity. But make sure you genuinely want the item and would be delighted to have it.

30 March   *Decorate your work space.* **Make it** look just like you want it to look. It doesn't matter whether your spot is a desk in the hallway or a thousand-square-foot corner office. Make it look like you, like you live there. Set it up to be the best environment for you to perform at peak efficiency.

If your work situation permits, put up pictures, bring in plants, and get the kind of furniture that makes your office as efficient and comfortable as possible. Money doesn't have to be a barrier. You can get used rugs, couches, and chairs for reasonable prices. Put up inexpensive posters of France, or cats, or flowers.

Make your space a place to which you want to come and work. See how much more productive you are once it looks the way you want it to. Are the files in the right place? Do you have enough pictures of your husband and kids? Did you hang your diplomas and degrees? Did you put up the award you won last year for having made the most sales in the month of April? As you look around, your office should be a reflection of you, your personality, and your accomplishments.

31 March *Do whatever you feel like doing.* Forget completely about what you should do, what others expect of you, what your obligations are. Spend the day as if no outside authority exists, as if you are 100 percent the master of your own fate, that you control your time, attention, effort.

How would you spend your day? Would you go to work? If you do, what will you work on? Do only what you want to do. If you don't want to go to work, stay home and do whatever you want. Putter around. Read the newspaper from cover to cover. Catch up with correspondence. This day belongs completely to you. You don't have to answer to anyone else for your time.

Do this moment to moment. If you start something and you don't want to finish it, put it down. Don't feel compelled to do anything you don't want to do. Don't even get out of bed if you don't want to! You control your life. There is no outside authority. You are in charge. There are no excuses for not doing exactly what you've wanted to do but haven't found the time for. Today you've found it.

Happiness Is Individual

This is easier to overlook than you think. What makes your spouse, your neighbor, your best friend, or your assistant happy will not necessarily make you happy. Although on the face of it this is an obvious consideration, it is tempting to fall into patterns of behavior that do not and will not work for you simply because you cannot resist the pressure, sometimes subtle and sometimes overt, to conform.

We all live within a network of influence that includes friends, family, colleagues, school, and place of worship, and beyond these immediate influences are the nation, the media, and the world at large. Each of these elements has expectations of us, sometimes consistent, sometimes contradictory, but always powerful.

Yet at the same time, there is no one exactly like you, never has been, never will be. The happiest people are those who recognize that their happiness is *their* happiness, not their father's, or their Aunt Mary's, or their boss's, or their senator's, or the guy's on TV in the commercial telling you that brand X just won't do the same for you as brand Y.

The quality of my own happiness shot up like a rocket when I realized that I didn't have to live anyone else's life, that what I wanted to do was valid and legitimate, even if others found it "weird" or "unorthodox" or "radical." When I recognized that I didn't have to play corporate politics, purchase my happiness, or acknowledge any external limitations, I stopped living a lie.

The task in life (and that task is an exciting, marvelous, surprising experience) is to find out who you are and *be that person.* What makes you literally jump for joy? What gets your adrenalin pumping so that you feel like popping out of your skin, that you can't sit still or not share your feeling because it is so overflowing that your own body can't contain it? You know when it's there. You don't need anyone to tell you how you feel about something, whether it draws or repels you, whether it makes you deliriously happy or puts you to sleep.

If you keep your inner eye on your life, both the individual elements and the broader whole, you'll more quickly develop a sense of where you want to be, with whom, and doing what.

April

1 April, April Fool's Day *Surprise someone.* Do something that will catch your target completely unawares. Show up at your girlfriend's house at 7:00 A.M. with flowers, croissants, and a fresh pot of coffee, or thoroughly clean your teenager's room before he gets home from school.

This surprise could be big or small, planned or completely spontaneous. But make sure the person about whom you are thinking has no idea of what you've planned, and that she will remember every April Fool's Day forevermore because the surprise is so out of character for you.

Pick up your husband at work, drive to a beach or lake, and spend the rest of the afternoon or evening together, reminiscing about all you've been through. If you normally visit your parents every Friday night for dinner, go there today and take them out to their favorite restaurant. This is a day to be creative about life. Imagine all the possibilities, then choose the one act that has you written all over it.

2 April *Learn a new dance.* Think of a dance you have always liked, or one about which you've just heard, and learn how to do it.

There are literally dozens to choose from. You can move from the Latin dances like samba, mambo, and tango, to ballroom dances like the fox-trot, polka, and box step, to western dances like the square dance and country swing.

Anyone can learn to dance. The idea of having two left feet is a myth. Everyone has rhythm and can be taught to move to a beat with a partner.

Learning the new steps and movement of a dance is both a discipline and a release. Moving in a patterned way induces a sense of control, yet also provides an opportunity for creative expression. It is also a great way to connect with someone you've never met before, or have been married to for twenty-five years.

3 April   *Get dirty.* Get involved with anything that will soil your hands and/or clothes. Garden, change the chain on your bicycle, or feed a two-year-old. Go to the beach, lie near the water, and cover yourself head to toe with sand, or visit a kiddie park and play in the sandbox.

Make very effort to get dirt on yourself. The point here is to get dirty, not avoid getting dirty. Wear some old clothes that you don't care about and wallow in mud. Strip and paint an old table, change the oil in your car, or clean out the attic. Look around and select the dirtiest job you can think of, then get into it.

When you finish, clean yourself off lovingly and carefully. Wash your body from head to toe, clean or polish your fingernails, and look with pride at the job you've just completed.

4 April *Acknowledge people who serve you.* Make sure you tell them how much you appreciate that they are there to help you find something, answer a question you may have, give you directions, ring up your groceries, or deal with you over the phone.

Make sure your response has nothing to do with the quality of service they have provided. Even if they have not done a particularly good job, acknowledge them anyway. Even the surliest attendant at the tollbooth gets a "Thank you, have a nice day." No act of service is too small to acknowledge. The elevator operator gets acknowledged. The person who waits on you, takes your coat, asks you to fill out an application, hands you your dry cleaning, anyone who makes it possible for you to get through your day receives an acknowledgment.

And if someone's service is outstanding, spare no praise. Here's your opportunity to let him really know how much you appreciate what he's done for you—even if you're paying for it.

5 April *Make your baseball predictions.* Make sure you do this before the start of the season. You can meticulously analyze every team and try to figure out which ones are going to do well, or, if you don't know anything about baseball, write them down at random.

It's best to do this with a partner. After you've written down your predictions, compare them and talk about how you arrived at your decisions. Baseball is a game that prompts discussion, so offer reasons why you think a certain team will do well and another poorly. It might help to have last year's standings or the results of the exhibition games on hand.

At the end of the season, see how well you did. Devise a point system to rate your predictions. Then add up the points and see who proved the best seer. Without knowing anything about the teams, you might do just as well as a baseball buff. That's just the way the game is.

6 April   *Enroll in a class that interests you.* There are adult classes given everywhere, at all times of the year. Find out if a class is being offered nearby that you'd want to take, and enroll.

Have you been thinking about becoming an importer/exporter? There are people who will be glad to tell you everything you need to know. Are you interested in photography? What kind? Black and white or color? Do you want to print the photos yourself? Decide what area you would like to deepen your knowledge of and take a course.

Would you love to know how to ride a horse? It's not as difficult as you may think. Look around for a class. In a short period of time you'll move rapidly up the learning curve. In a matter of weeks you'll be amazed at how much more you can do.

7 April *Prepare a meal you've never cooked before.* Start with an appetizer, go on to the main course, and finish up with dessert. If you're feeling ambitious, if you know you're going to make the most scrumptious dinner imaginable, invite some guests to share the feast.

Go through your cookbooks and see what looks good. Are there recipes you've been thinking about making for years and haven't gotten around to? Is there a dish you had at a friend's house recently, or at a restaurant, that you'd like to make yourself? Do it. Have no fear. If you feel you want to improvise, go ahead. If the recipe calls for basil and you're convinced oregano would work better, now's the time.

You can either tell your guests that you're cooking all new things and ask them if they'd be up for an experimental meal, or you can say nothing. Just invite them for dinner, serve the meal, watch their faces light up as they devour every morsel of your linguine alle vongole or chicken Kiev, receive their deepest compliments with gratitude, and then casually inform them that you've never tried any of the dishes they've just eaten.

Then notice their mouths fall open as they blink at you with incredulity. Ask them to do the same for you with their favorite new recipes. They might jump at the chance to reciprocate.

8 April   *Stretch and breathe.* These are obviously two activities you perform every day, but today do them with deliberation and purpose.

The best time to stretch and breathe is when you wake up, before you eat breakfast. Find a quiet spot, one that is warm enough for you to do these stretching/breathing exercises wearing your most comfortable clothes. Then gently stretch your body, slowly breathing in and out through your nose as you stretch.

One beneficial stretching position is to form an inverted V with your hands and legs. Place your hands on the floor and keep your legs straight. Hold the position for four counts, then slowly come up. Feel your limbs stretch and the blood oxygenate your brain as it fills up your head.

Be aware of your limbs, your muscles, your joints. Don't stretch too far. As soon as you feel resistance, pause, breathe in, and then stretch another quarter inch or so as you breathe out.

When you finish, lie peacefully on your back for several minutes. Darken the room and cover yourself with a light blanket or towel. Shut out the world for a spell. Think about nothing. Let your mind drift.

9 April   *Walk in the rain.* If the day turns out sunny, wait for the next rainy day. Invite a friend to go along or take your spouse and children with you. Whether the precipitation is light mist or a torrential downpour, feel the sensation of being exposed to the elements and the comfort of being prepared for them at the same time.

Get all bundled up and make sure you have the right kind of rain gear. Wear boots and raincoats and hats and take umbrellas if you like, and merrily walk along as if the sun were shining and the temperature were seventy-four degrees. You don't have to be out all day. An hour will do. Even fifteen minutes will work if you're not so sure about doing this at all.

Smell the moist, humid air, and the fragrance of spring bursting forth. Think about the fact that the water coming down on you is part of a continuing cycle of precipitation, evaporation, condensation, and more precipitation. The falling rain is as old as the universe itself. The same amount of water exists today as has always existed, more or less.

10 April   *Make a flower arrangement.* Even if you've never done anything with flowers but buy them and give them to someone else, get several different types of flowers and put together a bouquet with the artistry a professional would employ.

Choose your flowers on the basis of color, texture, shape, size, and durability. Ask your local florist about the different properties of the flowers, which ones commonly go together, which ones last the longest, which ones are most fragrant.

See the flower arrangement as a work of art, as a way of creatively expressing your unique and individual sense of form, of doing something you might never have done before and probably thought you couldn't do. Look at a few books on floral arrangement for suggestions.

Make sure the vase in which you place the flowers does justice to your arrangement. You don't have to use more than eight or ten flowers to create something truly magnificent. When you're finished, put the work of art in a place where you can really enjoy it—on the breakfast table or your desk at work, and stop and smell the flowers whenever the desire moves you.

11 April *Imagine a genie has emerged from Aladdin's lamp and will grant you three wishes.* What would they be?

The genie says she's not sure she'll get around to you any time soon, so you have to be certain your wishes are enduring desires, not just passing fancies.

The genie also says she'll come back at the end of the day to listen to your requests, so you have the rest of the day to think about it. What do you want? What do you REALLY want? Because whatever it is, it's yours.

Fame, fortune, good health, a lean, strong body, a new house, blond hair, kids who are well behaved, a boss who recognizes your abilities. . . . Think deeply. Whatever it is, it's as easy as saying the words.

At the end of the day, write these three wishes down and look at them frequently. Be careful of what you ask for. You usually get it!

12 April   *Attend a baseball game.* If you live in or near a major league city, go to the ballpark. If not, you can attend a minor league game, a college game, or even a Little League game.

Make sure the weather is sunny on the day you go. Get other people to go with you, including kids if you like, and sit out there as if there were nothing else going on in your life. Buy hot dogs and peanuts and beer and ice cream, or pack a lunch, and watch the national pastime being played by young multimillionaires.

Get into the rhythm of the game. Slow down to its pace. See how the action takes time to develop. Watch the individual duel between pitcher and batter. See the coaches give the signals as the batter briefly steps out between pitches.

Ruminate on whatever comes into your mind during the game. The ballpark is an excellent place to ponder the meaning of life, or think about nothing in particular.

13 April   *Start a book club.* Invite some friends or relatives whose intellectual or literary predilections appeal to you, and ask if they'd like to become charter members of the "It Meets Every Third Wednesday of the Month" book club.

At your first meeting, discuss the type of club you want to have. You can choose a selection committee, or rotate the choices every month. Is there a permanent group leader, or does the one who chose the book lead the parade? Are you going to read fiction, nonfiction, or a little of each?

Make sure that people who have not finished or even read the book feel comfortable at the meetings. No guilt trips. If you want extremes of opinion to set up a debate, let the most vociferous backer and critic start out, then let everyone else have his or her turn.

Plan for a one-hour discussion, then adjourn for refreshments. Make it a social gathering. Do it as much for the camaraderie as for the books themselves. Decide upon your new members policy. Do you let anyone in, or does an additional member have to be sponsored?

Make sure your selections are readily available in paperback. Once your system is agreed upon, implement a rule that no one in the group can take a potshot at the system until the group has met at least three times.

14 April *Meditate.* Set aside twenty to thirty minutes, find a quiet, comfortable spot, and wear loose clothing that doesn't bind you anywhere.

Sit with a straight spine and your legs folded. (Imagine a string like a puppet's extending from the top of your head.) Put on some soft music, close your eyes, and concentrate on a small, imaginary red spot between and slightly above your eyes.

At first, your mind will feel like it's racing at a thousand miles an hour and everything you've thought about for the past two weeks is passing through. Don't panic. And don't suppress anything that comes up. Let your mind go.

Also, don't dwell on anything. Let it pass. Pretend your mind is a television screen that projects images of its own choosing. That's its job. After a few minutes you'll become aware of your mind starting to slow down. Maintain the same posture. Just let the thoughts come to you. If you have to shift your body position, do so.

Don't think about what's coming through. Pretend it's being flashed through someone else's mind. Don't put any judgments on your thoughts.

After ten or fifteen minutes of meditation, gradually bring yourself back to full awakeness, become aware of your body and surroundings, and slowly get on with your day.

15 April   *Account for everything you value.* Go through all your possessions, your papers, personal articles, valuables, and make sure you know the status of these items. Where are they? Does each of them have a place? Do you know where to find them? If there is a book you particularly cherish and you've lent it to someone, do you know where it is, and do you have a plan to have it returned to you?

If you value your car, do you maintain it properly, or is it all banged up and about to burn its last drop of motor oil? What about gifts you've received over the years? Do you take care of them? Do you use them? If not, consider giving the gifts to someone who you know will cherish them.

What about personal relationships? Which ones are the most valuable to you? Do you nurture them, cultivate them, do whatever you have to do to be an exemplary friend, daughter, husband, supervisor? Do you demonstrate how much you value the relationship through your actions, your words, and your motivations?

16 April   *Vary your exercise.* If you regularly work out, add a new exercise to your repertoire. Do you run? Ride a bicycle. Do you already ride a bicycle? Take a long walk. Do you already have a walking routine? Swim at the local pool.

As you perform this new movement, see if you pick up the rhythm right away, or if it takes some time to adjust to the novelty. Are you using the same muscle groups, or do you feel soreness in parts of your body you never noticed before?

If you're not exercising at all, start today.

17 April *Visit a museum.* Art, science, natural history, historical, local—decide which one appeals to you.

Ask someone to go with you, or take your family if that works. You don't have to stay all day, and you don't even have to move through the museum at the same pace. Just concentrate on what you're interested in, and stay with that for as long as you like.

If nothing appeals to you, keep moving. Don't stay with anything because you feel you must. Museums are like buffets: Inside there's a wide range from which to choose, but you don't have to eat everything. If you see a van Gogh that appeals to you, linger with it for a long time. Examine the texture, the representation, the way color and stroke are an integral part of the composition.

As soon as you feel you've seen or heard enough, leave. If there are things you feel you missed, or would like to explore further, go again soon.

18 April *Do something you know is excessive, but do it without guilt.* Eat a pint of ice cream all by yourself, or buy several pastries and have them for lunch.

Enjoy every bite. Let go of the part of you that criticizes yourself for being "bad." Indulge your desires. Stay up all night. Go shopping instead of going back to work in the afternoon, or shoot pool all day.

Act on your fantasies. Pretend you've never heard of the word "moderation." Go overboard with your actions, but make sure you recognize that you have chosen to do this. No one is forcing you, and no one will censor you for your behavior. You are an adult, and in control of your life. Remember— no guilt, just pure enjoyment.

19 April *Attend or rent a foreign movie.* Make sure it's not dubbed, but has English subtitles. As you watch the film, become aware of the differences between your own culture and the one portrayed on the screen. It doesn't matter whether the movie is in French, Italian, Japanese, Spanish, or Russian, or where it was made.

Note the difference in the way people look, how they stand, their facial expressions and mannerisms. What matters to them? Is it the same or different from what matters to you? Can you follow their motivations, or are they completely alien to your experience?

How does the language of the film sound to your ear? Pleasant? Sexy? Incomprehensible? Forbidding? Do the actors remind you of people you know, or are you unable to relate to them?

Think about how the movie ends. Try not to focus on whether you liked the movie, but what you thought of the world you just glimpsed.

20 April *Clean your house or apartment from top to bottom.* Do a real spring cleaning. Make it a family project, assign tasks to all members, and do nothing today but make your living space spotless.

Pull back the beds and dust where you haven't looked in years. Wash the windows. Polish the silverware. Take down all the pictures and anything else that hangs on your walls and clean the glass and the frames. Every area of your home that you've neglected lately should get full attention.

When you're finished, celebrate your new, spotless home in a special way. Open a bottle of champagne, take pictures of your place as it looks right now, or linger in each room, noticing how everything sparkles.

21 April   *Look a homeless person in the eye.*
You don't have to give him money, or even talk to him. Just
acknowledge his existence by making eye contact.

If you smile at him as well, even the vaguest, faintest
smile, it might be the kindest action anyone has taken
toward him in ages. You validate your own humanity by vali-
dating someone else's, especially someone whose humanity
has all but been extinguished.

22 April   *Do something you've been wanting or
meaning to do but haven't.* Regardless of the reason you
haven't done it, do it today.

Have you been dreaming about telling the woman at the
train station that she has the most beautiful face you've
ever seen? Just walk right up to her and say, "You know,
Denise, I've been wanting to say this to you for the longest
time. You are so lovely you make my knees weak."

Doing something you've been reluctant to do will show
you—once you do it—how easy it really is, that you are often
not as timid as you thought you might be, or not even timid
at all. Is there a pair of shoes you've had your eye on and just
didn't think you could really buy, that they might not be you?
Go ahead, do it. Wear them. Talk about them. Solicit com-

ments. See yourself differently as a result of doing something you never thought you could do, at least not right now.

Then start thinking about the next life challenge you might undertake.

23 April *Let everyone go ahead of you.* Whether you are driving, waiting to use the copy machine at work, getting into line at the supermarket, or leaving a restaurant at lunchtime, let everyone you encounter go in front of or get served before you.

Drive as if everyone else has the right of way. Stop for pedestrians. Let people change lanes in front of you without difficulty. When the deli man barks, "Who's next?" point to the person beside you and say, with a smile, "He is."

Make sure you let these people know you're deliberately deferring to them. Don't pretend you're just being indecisive or weak, but rather that your sense of courtesy is so refined that you look for opportunities to exercise it. In most cases, you don't even have to say anything. Use hand gestures to allow people ahead of you, and watch for their reactions.

24 April *Imagine something wonderful.* It could be anything, as long as it's a fantasy spun out of your imagination. Concentrate on making what you imagine as

real as possible. Think of sensations, shapes, textures, temperatures, the person or persons you're with, the feeling you get when you place yourself in this fantasy.

The fantasy could be personal, professional, or global. Do you wish for peace on earth, that everyone had a decent home and enough to eat? Imagine how you will feel if that were to materialize, how differently people would behave, what their priorities would be.

Do you long for a job change? Imagine asking your boss for some of her time; tell her you'd like to share some thoughts you have about your work. Then see yourself going in, sitting down, going over all that you've accomplished over the year, and asking to be promoted, with a new title and office. Then imagine your boss, with a huge smile on her face, agreeing with you wholeheartedly, telling you it's a pleasure to reward such a productive employee, that she wishes all her employees were equally effective.

Keep this or any other scene in mind constantly, and return to it whenever you have a moment or two to think about whatever it is you want. Elaborate on your vision. See it as already having happened.

25 April *Go hunting for bargains.* If this activity is already part of your normal routine, see if you can take your skill to the next level, if you can really perfect the art of finding the best possible items at the lowest possible prices.

The way to have some fun with this suggestion is to organize a party. Invite friends to join you on this expedition. Ask everyone to suggest places to visit, and look in the newspaper or neighborhood shopper for advertised specials. Make sure you set a limit for yourself. You can also decide ahead of time if you want to buy a few special things or go for quantity. Either will work.

Don't accept every markdown you see. Some stores offer discounts on merchandise they've recently marked up, so be careful. Ask the person who serves you what he or she would recommend. A well-informed salesperson can be a valuable asset and contribute to the success of the day. You don't have to spend money in every location. In fact, it might make sense to look around first and then return to the store that offers the best deals.

Many stores do not allow returns or refunds on reduced merchandise, so if you're unsure about something it makes sense to have in mind a friend or relative to whom you could give the item in case it's the wrong fit or color.

At the end of the day you can splurge on something you wouldn't have gotten had you paid full price for what you bought earlier.

26 April   *Do something for someone as if you were doing it for yourself.* Offer to take on a project for a friend or relative, and carry it out as if you were the beneficiary.

Perform the task or activity with as much care as you can. The challenge is to treat someone to your best possible work.

There is a folk tale out of the Middle Ages that illustrates the point. A wealthy man went to his friend, a builder, and asked him to build the best house possible. He told him to spare no expense, that he would be paid for the time and the materials it took. The builder, who was not a wise man, saw an opportunity to take advantage of his wealthy friend. Instead of using the finest materials and craftsmen, he used the cheapest and least experienced. Instead of taking his time, the builder rushed through the project, building a ramshackle dwelling whose attractive exterior hid inferior work.

When the house was finished, he charged the wealthy man as though he had followed his instructions. The man thanked the builder, paid the full amount, then handed over the key to him, saying that he was giving the builder the house as a gift. The startled builder was suddenly the recipient of his own shoddy effort.

The moral of the story is obvious: You never know when something you do for someone else is really being done for yourself. Do your best for others.

27 April
Tell someone you love him or her. It could be someone who obviously knows you love her, or someone who doesn't, or even someone who isn't quite sure. The point is to speak, to say the words.

You can't beat around the bush by sending candy with a note that says "I Love You" on it. You also can't get by on this one by merely telling yourself that you love someone and letting it go at that. Telling someone that you love him, someone who doesn't hear it very often from you, strengthens the bond that already exists between you, or creates a bond if you've never uttered the three magic words to this person before.

Don't worry about the other person's reaction. Some people will tell you right back that they love you, some people will be embarrassed by your outward show of affection, and others will pretend that they didn't hear you. But regardless of the reaction, no one will fail to be affected by your declaration, from your young granddaughter, to your mother, to the guy you've been dating for a while and to whom you've wanted to say some of the most important words in the world.

28 April   *Do a complete makeover.* Look completely different at the end of the day from the way you looked at the beginning.

Start with a new haircut. Cut off that mess with which you've been walking around, decide on a chic new "do" from photographs of how they're wearing their hair in Paris, change your color, and tell your hairdresser or barber that if people recognize you after you leave the shop, you want your money back.

After the brand-new haircut, move on to your clothes. Get a whole new outfit, one that is definitely not the you you were up until today. Make sure that what you buy makes a statement about yourself you've never made before. If it's appropriate, also have your makeup done differently.

See how far you'll go with yourself today. See what your limits are. Test your ability to stretch what you think you're capable of doing. If you want to keep going, try a new pair of glasses.

29 April *Avoid profanity.* If occasions arise in which your impulse is to use obscene language, try to stop yourself before you utter the words. Pretend that you have no knowledge of those words, that your vocabulary doesn't include them. Express strong emotions that arise—fear, surprise, excitement, disappointment—through some other means, like gestures, facial expressions, or other verbal exclamations.

Be extremely polite. Say *please* and *thank you* in every situation that calls for it. And say it with conviction and sincerity. Mean it. Don't fail to demonstrate your ability to be polite even once.

If this is the way you normally are, if you would never think of using profanity, congratulate yourself for the proper, considerate manner with which you deal with people and situations. If you are prone to stronger reactions, see if you can go one day gracefully, politely acknowledging the existence of etiquette by practicing it.

30 April *Barter with someone for something you want, by giving up something you could easily part with.* Bartering is a great way of realizing that you can get things you desire without having to buy them, that items and talents already in your possession can be vehicles for obtaining new things.

Is there a bicycle sitting idly in your garage, collecting dust, while you spend your winters on skis and your summers sailing? Perhaps a friend of yours has two tickets to a show that she'd like to trade for the bicycle. Don't worry that the original prices may be disparate, or that the current values are not equal. Think of it as an even trade. Think of the pleasure you would get out of this deal, and that what you propose to give up is not something you use very much.

You can also trade services. Take stock of what you could do for someone in exchange for something you'd like done. Is housekeeping not in your budget, although you'd love to have someone come in every week and clean your place properly? Call a few housekeepers and see which ones are open to trading. Can you give a manicure and pedicure? Do you teach the violin? Will you babysit her kids or walk her dog?

Barter gets you in touch with the past, before there was money, when trading was the primary way in which economic life was conducted. It's a great way to reduce your dependence on cash and enjoy things you might not otherwise be able to afford.

Is Anyone Happy
All the Time?

In the course of researching the question of happiness, through countless discussions over the past twenty years, I've been asked one question over and over: "Are you happy all the time?" The answer is a resounding no.

In many ways, it's counterproductive to make constant happiness your goal. For one thing, it's dishonest, because you'll find yourself having to lie to both yourself and others to maintain that standard. For another thing, it places much too high an expectation on you right from the start. It's like the person who starts diet after diet and then gives them up just as frequently because he or she has "cheated."

It is not necessary, or even desirable, to be happy all the time to be an essentially happy person. I experience my share of pique, frustration, disappointment, discomfort, displeasure, fitfulness, miscommunication, and impatience. But what I have also developed is the ability to be aware of my condition, to know its origins, and to take measures, when appropriate, to change my reality. I am not a victim of circumstances. I do not choose to abdicate my responsibility for my own pleasure. It is my responsibility, and my happiness resides in that awareness and in the actions that result from that awareness.

A happy person is not someone to whom "bad" things do not happen, or who ignores the negative in some kind of forced reverie that more resembles Pollyanna than anything real or human. Rather, it is someone who understands that his or her *reactions* to events—not the external conditions that are subject to the vagaries of many conflicting forces, most of which are out of our control—are the stuff of happiness.

May

1 May   *Read about a miracle.* While the miracles in the Bible are certainly appropriate, you might want to focus on something more modern, to strengthen the credulity of the miracle because of its unexpectedness; after all, the Bible was written in the Age of Miracles.

How is it that people in India eat glass, or that you can run across glowing hot coals at 1500°F and not burn yourself, or that a person can fall 10,000 feet from an airplane in an unopened parachute and survive with a few broken bones? When you read about this miracle, determine why you think it qualifies. Does it defy the laws of logic? Is it something that modern science cannot explain? Are you satisfied that the facts are correct? If the miracle really piques your interest, see if you can learn about additional miracles.

Ask people you know if they've heard of any miracles, and talk to them about the ones you've been studying. Think about what kind of miracle you would like to have happen in your life. Research this particular miracle and find out if it's happened to other people.

On three separate occasions, six years apart, a ring that was given to me for my thirteenth birthday was lost as it flew off my hand in the act of throwing a ball. I found it the first time in sandy soil, feeling with my hands as darkness set in; the second time in a field covered with autumn leaves; and the third time when a sliver of it was still visible after a truck had run over it, driving it into the asphalt street. I still have the ring, although, not willing to tempt fate again, I no longer wear it.

2 May *Take a nap in the afternoon.* Rearrange your schedule so that you can get some uninterrupted time. Take off an afternoon from work if you have to, and make sure you get this respite before the kids, your spouse, or your roommate comes home from school or work.

Find a quiet, comfortable spot in a familiar place. Your living room couch is probably the best place to be right now. Make sure you don't have anything going on in your mind that would prevent you from submitting to sleep. Unplug your phone. Put on some quiet music, or pick up a book or magazine, and devote all your attention to what you're listening to or reading.

Within minutes you should be asleep. You can sleep for as long as you'd like. Even a twenty-minute nap will be enough to refresh you. But if you want to sleep for two hours, and you have the time, go right ahead. If you're reading, as soon as you feel your eyes getting drowsy, just lay the book or magazine down on your stomach as you lie on your back.

Chances are you'll sleep deeply and wake up as if you've just spent an entire night in bed—refreshed, alert, focused, energetic, and ready to spend the second half of the day productively.

3 May   *Speak with precision.* Make sure every word you utter today is exactly what you want to say. Don't waste any words. Don't talk for the sake of talking, or to fill up time, or because you are uncomfortable with silence. Use words as an extraordinary way of communicating complex human thoughts and emotions.

This might mean slowing down the process, thinking before you speak, listening more carefully than you normally do, and pausing to choose the right word or phrase. Don't try to sound important, or dazzle someone with your vocabulary, or approximate what you mean to say and figure, "Aw, what the heck, it's close enough."

If you want to convey to someone that an event in your life was significant, say "significant," not "big." Cut out all "likes," "you knows," and "reallys." Pretend you had a limit on the number of words you could use and you didn't know what that limit was. Use words sparingly, but with meaning and emotion to elaborate on the intended purpose of your speech. Using gestures to communicate more completely will help cut down on the number of words required to get your point across.

4 May   *Play catch.* Get a ball, invite a friend or two along, go out to your backyard, a park, or the street in

front of your house or apartment, and throw the ball back and forth.

Throw pop-ups. Throw grounders. Throw it hard. Throw it soft. Talk about anything that appeals to you.

If you have small children, you can get a spongy, colorful ball and form a circle. Get two balls and have two catches simultaneously. See if you can make the balls hit in midair. Play wire ball, step ball, or make up a game. Throw with the hand you don't normally use. Catch with only one hand. Be creative. Make up games as you go along.

5 May   *Sit in a café.* If the weather is nice, sit outside. The point of this activity is to while away time, to let minutes, even hours pass without caring how that time is being spent.

Order a coffee, cappuccino, iced tea, or beer, and just sit. You can read a newspaper, magazine, or book; write a letter or make an entry in your journal; or spend the time watching people.

Sitting in a café can be done with a friend, although before you invite someone make sure he or she is simpatico. Practice the art of conversation, daydream, watch the action on the street, or do a little of everything.

If you go alone, and the mood strikes you, find someone who looks interesting and ask that person if you can join him. Compliment him on something and begin a conversation. Remember, you are not on an airplane. You can get up and leave at any time. Make sure you like the feeling of the spot you choose. If you do, come back again. If you don't, try another place. Visit a number of cafés and see what the differences are in ambience, clientele, service, food, etc.

If this activity appeals to you, develop a favorite hangout.

6 May   Invite an unusual guest to dinner. Go out of your way to think of someone whom you or your family would not expect to find at the dinner table, and invite him or her. You don't have to make anything special; your everyday cooking will do just fine. What's important is that the person is outside of your normal intimate setting, but is someone you'd either like to know better or want to thank for having been kind or generous to you.

Can you think of a particularly difficult situation with which someone recently helped you? Did someone go to bat for you on a car loan? Is there an individual with whom you regularly interact on a business level that you're itching to get to know better? Invite her for dinner. It will totally change the interaction that goes on that night at the dinner table. Everyone in your household will be more alert, will want to be on his or her best behavior to impress your guest. Your relationship with your guest will change as well.

If you dine alone, this is an opportunity to show your guest how naturally you can prepare a meal. Or if you want, you can forget about your normal dining routine and practice putting together an evening that will dazzle your visitor.

7 May   *Be someone on whom nothing is lost.* For one day, be a sponge. Absorb everything that occurs. Imagine you have grown antennae and that nothing comes into your personal space without being recorded. Pay extra attention to what everyone says to you, and respond fully and clearly.

Make your own communication strong, direct, and honest. Make sure what you're putting out is exactly what you intend.

Novelist Henry James was challenged by a critic who claimed that his characters were not believable, that they were people on whom nothing was lost, and real people weren't like that. James replied, "Yes, but they should be."

Try to be a character of whom James would be proud. See if you can even pick up the thoughts and feelings of others. See if you can tune into what's *not* being said, picking it up as clearly as if it were being broadcast over a loudspeaker.

8 May   *Start a journey in your mind.* Sit quietly in a comfortable position. Breathe deeply and slowly. Become aware of every breath, the way your chest fills up with air, and how your stomach feels when you let it out. When you feel the rhythm of your breathing, let go of thought and allow yourself to drift.

You can travel by any mode of transportation. You can even fly. Imagine yourself on this journey, going by whatever means—foot, bicycle, boat, car, train, animal, plane, motorcycle—suits you at each moment.

Where are you going? Who is with you? What do you see along the way? The vast blueness of the ocean, the quiet of a meadow high up in the mountains, the nervous excitement of the center of a big city? Stay where you have traveled for as long as you want. There is no hurry to leave. You can come and go as you please. The world you inhabit is the world you have created. There is no other reality.

Are you climbing in the Himalayas, or sipping a daiquiri while the warm ocean laps at your feet in the Hawaiian Islands? Think about how you feel being there. What lessons are yours and yours alone to learn? Ask yourself to provide the answers. Stay on your journey until you find the perfect destination, then slowly leave your spot and return to your point of origin, and then to your body.

9 May　*Be extra efficient with time.* Don't waste a moment. Make each action accomplish more than one thing. Play a game with yourself. See how many projects you can complete in the shortest time possible. Challenge yourself to figure out more and more ways of becoming efficient.

See how long it takes you to do things with this thought in mind. You can easily determine if you are wasting time in your life by becoming more aware of how long it takes you to do everyday things. While you are brushing your teeth, think about what you are going to get done today. As you drive to work, picture yourself completing your first task. Don't wait around for the coffee to drip at the coffee machine. Wait until it's already made and go back. On your way to and from the machine, drop off memos or communicate a message to a co-worker.

Don't hurry. There's no need to rush through things. Work smarter, not harder. Just be aware of what you're doing. See if you feel like you accomplished more today in a shorter amount of time. Think about incorporating some of the techniques you employed today into your everyday routine.

10 *May*   *Write a speech.* Perhaps you are actually in a position to deliver it, perhaps not; that's not important. If you can deliver it, write it so that people will actually hear it. If you haven't got an audience, imagine any situation in which you would have to speak and write the speech for that situation. Imagine that you are the President of the United States and are speaking before the United Nations, or you've just won the Oscar for best actress and you're out there in front of the Academy and a hundred million people worldwide.

Jot down a few notes of the significant points you want to make. Just write down key words, phrases, and ideas. Keep that piece of paper at hand as you start to write your speech.

First you must develop rapport with your audience. Who are these people? What can you say to get to them quickly and easily? Do you know any jokes? Is there an anecdote or incident you can relate? What was the cab ride like on the way to your speech? Is there a story there?

Once you develop rapport with your audience, the rest is easy. People will be receptive to you. You can say just about anything and it will be well received. The opposite is also true. If you don't connect with your audience right away you might as well stand up there in silence, because they won't hear you.

Figure that you'll talk for about fifteen or twenty minutes maximum, at least to start. You'll probably go over that time, but if you plan for longer, your speech will drone on. Ask the audience a question. (That's always a good technique for connecting.) After you write and deliver your speech, answer questions from the audience, but take the time to elaborate on those you find most interesting.

11 May   *Watch a caterpillar transform itself into a butterfly.* If you don't have children, this might seem like something better left to a tenth-grade biology class, but what better way is there to observe the process of nature than to watch it taking place before your eyes?

There are, believe it or not, places from which you can buy caterpillars. These outlets will be able to tell you which one to buy, what to feed it, how to keep it, and what conditions to create. You might want to record this natural transformation by keeping a written record or taking pictures as the days pass.

Does your life feel any different, being involved so intimately in the transformation taking place before you? Does it humble you, or make you feel, as a human being, more powerful?

If you have children, how do they feel? Do they have sufficient reverence for nature? Do they have an appreciation for things less powerful, but no less marvelous, than they?

12 May   *If you weren't you, who would you be?* You could be this person for a day, a week, a year, or forever. Whose place would you like to take? Do you wish you were Charlie across the street because you can't take your eyes off his wife? Or would you rather be A. J. Foyt, about to race in the Indy 500?

Think about the qualities or circumstances of someone else's life that appeal to you, and why. The person doesn't even have to be alive. Could you see yourself as John Glenn, orbiting the earth for the first time? Would you want to be the pope? Or is Jane Fonda more your cup of tea?

What would you do first as this person? Would you change anything about him or her? If you could be Ivan Lendl, would you be more cheerful? If you could be Madonna, would you be more real? Think about the person you would become. Does that person exist? Would you create a totally new individual to fit the image you have of yourself? Would you be Michael Jordan, and play basketball as if it were your birthright? Or Bart Simpson, and be hipper than hip?

13 May   *Go on a picnic.* Organize your family, invite friends, and make this a special day. Ask everyone who's going what his or her favorite outdoor food is, have each bring it, and make your collective way out to a grassy spot.

Your picnic doesn't have to be far from home, although if you're ambitious and want to drive a long distance, feel free. Make sure there's enough sun and shade to allow everyone to be comfortable.

Spread out your blanket and open the picnic basket. Have everyone pitch in to help get the food ready, and notice what it feels like to have a meal among trees, near a stream, in view of mountains, by the side of a lake, or at the beach. Food always tastes better outdoors, so indulge in the pleasure of every morsel. Play a game or two. Badminton and volleyball are perfect picnic activities.

14 May   *Spend the entire day reading a book.* Make sure you can finish the book today because part of the pleasure of this activity is the feeling of accomplishment you get when you actually read the last page.

Your choice can be something you've read before, something you've been wanting to read, or a selection that just pops into your mind at the last minute. Get lots of sleep the night before and start on your book early, nesting in a comfortable spot. If it's a sunny day, reading outside would be ideal. Or you can read in bed, or on your favorite sofa.

If you aren't hooked on the book after about a half hour, put it down and make another selection. Don't read anything that doesn't appeal to you. That's a good rule of thumb for reading at any time. If the book grabs your attention, keep going. Take breaks only to eat and answer nature's call. Maybe you'll feel like dozing. That's okay, too.

Plan to finish the book in the early to mid-evening. If you finish by noon, pick up another one. If midnight rolls around and you're still reading, see if you can finish, but next time try a shorter book.

15 *May* *Go on a trip without a destination.* If you have a car, get in it, ask someone to go along with you if you like, and just start driving. If you don't have a car, take a bus or train, but don't decide where you're going. Just buy a ticket and start riding.

Once you're out on the road, or away from familiar surroundings, let your instincts guide you. If you like the name of an exit or a stop along the way, take it and follow it, or stay there for a while. See how it feels. If you like what you see, keep going. If not, get back on the road or the rails and move on.

Get a sense of your trip by staying in touch with your mood as you go along. At some points you might feel edgy or disoriented. Keep going. If you're feeling comfortable, this might be a place to stop, have a bite, and bathe in the local color.

You might want to make up a story about what you're doing. Are you looking for locations for a Hollywood movie? Perhaps you're out testing the direction of the wind for a new energy system. Whatever the case, spend the whole day just drifting, as if the entire country were your home, and you were merely visiting its farthest reaches without so much as a second thought.

16 May *Talk to an elderly person.* It could be a relative of yours, but if that's your choice, make sure you can have a lively conversation. Better yet, visit a retirement home and ask the staff to introduce you to a particularly lucid resident who is at least eighty years old.

Ask this man or woman about the way things used to be. Try to find out as much as you can about "the old days." What was it like to live through World War I and then the Roaring Twenties? Was the Great Depression as bad as people say? What things have surprisingly stayed the same? What things have changed the most?

Ask this person about his or her life. Where has he lived? How many children and grandchildren does she have, and where do they live? What's the most thrilling memory he has, and what has been her greatest disappointment? Does she have any regrets?

What does he think of things today? What has been gained? What has been lost? How would she like to be remembered?

There are an infinite number of questions that can give rise to a wonderful discussion between the two of you. And it will also provide an elderly person the opportunity to talk about his or herself in ways that are seldom, if ever, explored.

17 May *Order a gift for yourself from a catalog.* This can be one of the most fun (and is often one of the most overlooked) life experiences. You can spend $3 or $30,000, depending on your budget. There are things to buy that fit everyone's pocketbook.

First, get as many catalogs as you can reasonably go through. You can find them in the library, in stores, or you can call up mail-order houses and ask them to send you their catalogs. They'll be only too happy to oblige.

Then go through each one, looking at what it has to offer. It's okay to choose an item you can obtain at the corner store; the experience of buying through a catalog has pleasures all its own.

When you've chosen an item, you can either call the catalog's toll-free number or fill out the order form and write a check. Depending on the particular company, the item could be in your hands in a day or two months. But that's part of the fun—the anticipation of receiving something you've ordered and not knowing exactly when it will arrive, although you know it will.

Now's the time to order that carton of toilet tissue made from recycled paper, or the box of perfectly shaped pears. If you're feeling really indulgent, try the alpaca slippers.

When the item you settled on is delivered, the process of sending yourself a gift is complete.

18 May   *Visit a neighborhood in which you used to live.* This activity works best when you haven't lived there for a while, but it's fine to go back to a place that you left recently, too.

It would be a great adventure if your "old" neighborhood was in a different city, but this is not essential.

As you approach the streets with which you were once so acquainted, see if they look as familiar as you thought they would. Are there memories attached to them? Do you pass by your old grammar school? Is that where you first kissed Melissa Anderson, an innocent peck on the cheek that sent you into spasms of joy?

What does your old neighborhood look like now? Is it improved, or does it appear to be run-down? Do you have fond recollections of your street, or are they less than pleasant? As you pull up in front of your old house, see if you are motivated to ring the bell. If you are, and someone answers, tell him or her you used to live here and ask if you can go in and look around for a few minutes.

Does the house look the same, or does someone else's furniture make it look like you never lived there? Does the house have the same feeling as it once did for you?

Don't stay too long. As you drive away, think about how far you've come since you lived here.

19 May   *Get angry about something and let it go.* If something has been bothering you, get in touch with it. Don't suppress it or feel guilty about being angry over it. Give it a full airing.

Think about it. Talk about it. Write about it. Share it with someone who will listen to you, who will allow you to vent your feelings, who will be empathetic to your position, who will provide a perspective that you didn't see before.

You might even want to call the person at whom you are angry and let him or her know your feelings. Don't look for right or wrong. Don't feel your anger has to be justified. The point is to face it, embrace it, and erase it. Just say to the other person, "You know, it really hurt me when you didn't show up at Bobby's graduation. I know you had your reasons for missing it, but graduating from high school happens only once and Bobby wanted you to be there."

Once you've vented your feelings, resolve not to revisit this particular grievance. Life moves on. It's not something that will continue to slow you down. It's part of your experience; you've done your grieving, you've let it go, and now you're going to learn from it.

20 May *If you are already intimate with someone, make this a day of heightened sensuality. If you are unattached, use your imagination.*

Hook up with your partner at a time of the day that is agreeable, and plan to spend as much time as you can with him or her, exploring each other's bodies as you did when you first got together, when your interest in one another was at its height.

First, take a hot bath or shower together, soaping each other, and then carefully dry off with your thickest, plushest towels. You might want to share a glass of wine or a cup of tea to set your mood in the right direction.

Then get into bed and caress each other in long, slow, exaggerated movements, lovingly moving your hands in just the way that your lover adores. Feel the heightened sensuality, the way that time ceases when your conscious mind falls away and there is nothing but what's there before you, nothing but a moment that is both singular and eternal.

After making love, fall asleep in each other's arms, or lie awake and talk about things that people only share when they are exposed and vulnerable.

21 May *If you are unattached and desiring a partner, imagine the scenario under which you are meeting him or her.* Perhaps you have been invited to dinner at your best friend's house and, though when you first notice this stranger you're not immediately attracted, as the evening wears on he grows on you more and more. Maybe it's the way he smiles at you when he answers your questions, or offers to help wash the dishes after the meal has ended.

Imagine that he calls you a few days later. You feign mild surprise but deep down you've thought of nothing but him since you met. He asks you to dinner and you can see he is one to take things slowly, the way you like it.

The scenario can be different. You notice in your regular Wednesday night bowling league that the team three lanes over has a new member, and you marvel at her perfect form—her perfect bowling form that is. She seems so athletic and feminine at the same time. Your games are over but instead of going out for a beer with the guys you hang around and wait for her, introducing yourself and asking if she is unattached.

You have a cup of coffee and find that bowling is but one of many interests you share. You ask if you can see her again and she says, "Of course."

Imagining that you are meeting your true partner is entirely within your reach. Any situation is plausible. Keep imagining, and when you have met and are intimate with the man or woman of your dreams, go back and read yesterday's suggestion, although I doubt you'll need to.

22 May   *Don't watch any television.* Pretend that it doesn't exist, that you have never heard of it, that you just arrived from the planet Orth and it is inconceivable that you would sit all day in front of a box that talks and shows pictures.

If you share your home with others, try to get them to comply with your request not to watch any TV, and if you can't, then leave the house. If you find the notion implausible, that you wouldn't have the slightest idea of how to fill your time without television, then get a copy of Steve and Ruth Bennett's *365 TV-Free Activities,* or Frances Moore Lappé's *What to Do After You Turn Off the TV.*

Observe what life is like without the passivity that goes along with being a couch potato. Be active. Take the initiative. Read. Write. Take pictures. Sit out on the front porch and rock back and forth. No news. It doesn't exist. You're on your own. You have to provide your own entertainment because no one will do it for you.

23 May   *Make a tape for your grandchild or great-nephew.* You can do this even if you are sixteen years

old. Age is not a factor. The purpose of this activity is to communicate with someone close to you whom you don't even know yet, or who is too young to derive the wisdom you have to impart. Give your grandchild or future grandchild the benefit of what you know right now, your perspective on life from where you sit at this moment.

The tape can be audio or video, whichever is most convenient. It doesn't have to be long. Twenty to thirty minutes will do. Just sit and think about what you want someone fifty years from now to know, and record it.

When you're finished, put the tape in a safe place. If you have a safe-deposit box, put it in there and make sure you mention the tape in your will. Indicate when the tape is to be played, and for whom it's meant.

Add to your tape at any time. Or make a series.

24 May *Have a personal business card made.*
Actually, the card does not have to be about business at all if you have no business. Just have a calling card made that identifies you, that allows people to reach you at a later date if they're so inclined. This practice is common in other parts of the world. You'll meet someone, introduce yourselves, and then the person will give you a card with his name and phone number on it. That's it, just the name and phone number.

This is an opportunity to tell the world who you are by how you represent yourself graphically. It's not the same thing as a business card. That card is the image of the *busi-*

ness, not *you.* Even if you are the owner of your company, you still have to be conscious of the identity your company is putting out to the marketplace.

Not so with a personal card. You can be anybody. What's even better, you can be you. If you have the means, work with a graphic artist whose talent you respect. You can design the card yourself, or have a printer help you out. You can say anything you want on the card. You are giving yourself the opportunity to tell the world just who you are.

25 May *Spend the night in a new place, where you've never slept before.* This suggestion has many possibilities, ones that might call on you to be creative. The point here is not so much to sleep in a strange bed, although that certainly will be the result of carrying out this suggestion, but to experience a routine part of life differently.

You can go to a travel lodge, bed and breakfast, guest house, or cabin. You can camp out, backpack into the wilderness, or sleep in your own backyard. If you feel like having a pajama party, you can call your cousin and ask to sleep at her house. If you've been seeing someone and feel that tonight's the big night, make sure you do it at your partner's place.

Once you've chosen your venue, prepare for the adventure by packing what you need—anything from your toothbrush to complete bedding.

What does it feel like to sleep where you've never slept before? How does the sleeping surface compare to yours? Is it harder, or softer? Does it squeak? What are the pillows like? Did you bring yours? Are the arrangements for tomorrow's bath or shower taken care of? Will someone wake you up in the morning or are you on your own?

Sleeping in a strange place forces you to think about a variety of things that otherwise are as automatic as breathing. Every once in a while, it's great to make the strange familiar and the familiar strange.

26 May *Roll around on the floor with an infant.* Take off your shoes and get down to the baby's level.

Make sure the baby understands, through your body language as well as your words, that you two are equals, that you have entered his or her domain, and that you have chosen to do what the baby loves to do. Find a soft spot on the floor, cover it with blankets or comforters, and play his favorite music.

Be physical. Put the baby on top of you and hold him up in the air. Or hover over the baby while you coo, cuddle, and gently stroke or tickle him. Then place your head next to the baby's and look into his eyes, smile, and, in the high-pitched voice babies love to hear, ask him if he's having fun.

Chase the baby. If he crawls away, crawl after him. Catch up with him and then crawl around him. Make the baby change direction. If the baby doesn't crawl, gently roll around with him until he squeals with delight.

27 May   *Dine alfresco.* Pretend you're in a Mediterranean country, where eating outdoors is as natural as eating indoors in colder climates. If you need inspiration, rent a few Italian or French movies. Chances are there will be at least one scene in which a group of people sit down to a sumptuous outdoor feast. Or go to a bookstore and look through a beautiful cookbook for inspiration.

Invite friends or relatives to join you. It's okay to go to a park. A card table and a red-checkered tablecloth will create just the right atmosphere.

Prepare a meal that fits your budget. You might want to have wine, cheese, and green apples, so that your meal will be straight out of the European countryside. And have something chocolate for dessert.

How does the food taste? Do you find yourself eating more slowly, with more awareness of your surroundings? How about the conversation? Is it especially convivial?

This slight change can make an everyday activity something wonderful, something special, and you can do this whenever the weather permits.

28 May   *Listen to live music.* Call a friend or go with your partner to a place where your favorite kind of music is being played. If you can't find a place where you can

hear what you want today or tonight, plan for it by getting tickets to a performance in the future, or going on another evening.

You might want to get your eleven-year-old niece to give you a private recital on the violin. Or ask a friend who plays the piano if he wouldn't mind banging out a few tunes for you.

Each type of musical outing carries with it its own cultural peculiarities, so you'll have to think about how you're going to dress, what time you have to be in the hall, club, or park, and whether you can eat and drink during the performance. Live music gets you closer to the source of creativity, allows you to see how music is made. Watch for the expressions and body posture of the musicians. See how they relate to their instruments, what they do when they're not playing, and how you are moved by each piece.

29 May   *Don't waste anything.* Use only what you need, and be aware of what you're consuming so that your needs will be in line with the job you're doing.

You can start as soon as you get up in the morning. As you brush your teeth, turn off the water while you're brushing, and turn it on again when you're ready to rinse your mouth. Continue with the shower. Turn off the water as you soap. Or better yet, shower with your mate.

Turn off lights when you leave a room. Recycle paper, plastic, and metal whenever you can. Carpool to work.

Be sparing in your manner and speech. Don't waste your own time—or anyone else's.

30 May   *Float on a calm body of water.* Buy a plastic float at a nearby store, and head for your favorite water spot. It could be a lake, pond, stream, or swimming pool. Get a cold drink, load up on suntan lotion so you won't burn, hop on your float, and let go.

Feel the weight of your body being supported by the water. Relax your muscles, let go of any tension you may have, and just drift lazily along, slowly moving through the water without a care in the world. Try not to focus on anything but what comes into your mind naturally. Let your mind go as easily as you let your body go. When you close your eyes, imagine yourself gently floating in space.

Make sure you stay on your float long enough to feel that you've been on a voyage, that you've gone somewhere far away and that you have to return. See yourself as a traveler through time.

31 May   *Write a description of someone or something you love.* It doesn't have to be long, although feel free to go on at length if you choose. The important thing is

to think about this person, pet, or object so intently and insightfully that you can describe it thoroughly.

What if you want to describe your cat? How long are his whiskers? What are his eating and sleeping habits, his ways of responding? What is his demeanor with strangers, other cats, dogs? Does he like to be picked up and held? Is his hair short or long?

What about your toddler? Describe his size and shape, the way he moves, what his room looks like, what his favorite toys are and where he leaves them. What are the colors of his clothes?

Before you write, spend some time thinking about your subject. Form a mental image of this person or animal, or, if you want to describe your car, sit looking at it for a while. Keep this written description with the things you value, or write it into your journal.

Good Things Happen When You Expect Them To

It amazes me every time I encounter superstitions or old wives' tales that get in the way of good things happening, even though I grew up with them.

It has taken me a long time to realize that I was afraid to embrace my dreams for fear of warding them off with my confidence.

When I was growing up, we avoided speaking about what we longed for out of fear that focusing on it too much would "jinx" it. It was a complicated and very insidious way of dealing with life. You never spoke about what you wanted most. You erected great, elaborate defenses around your wishes and desires in order to stave off disappointment if they failed to materialize. I sometimes wondered why certain desired outcomes didn't happen even when I followed this course of avoidance (which was most of the time), but I never really challenged my outlook.

I now maintain that I compromised both my success and my happiness by negating that which I both knew I wanted and would make me happy. How can you attract something to yourself if you affect indifference and deny your wishes?

This mindset comes from the Judeo-Christian ethic of humbling yourself before God and being satisfied with what life provides you. Asking for what you want is considered arrogant, or overreaching. Remember what happened to Icarus, who flew too close to the sun, was punished by having the wax melt off his wings, and plummeted to his death.

But there is another part of the Western tradition that honors directness of purpose. "Ask and ye shall receive" is the part that rings true for me. What you want may not arrive in precisely the shape or form that you imagined, but it will surely fulfill your requirements. You only need to expect it to arrive at all, and affirm your intention to have it. With so much power at your disposal, why not use it?

June

1 June *Pick up every coin you see.* No coin is too small. No penny should go unnoticed.

Your prosperity depends, of course, on your ability to attract money, and when you stop to pick up whatever you see, you send out a message to the universe that you are open to receiving even more.

You'd be surprised at how much you can pick up in a day if you look for it. Pennies will eventually turn into nickels, dimes, and quarters, and then into bills.

If you put your mind to this task with persistence and consistency, you will start to attract larger sums, and then, before long, money will come pouring in from many sources. The key is to be open to receiving.

If you feel uneasy about picking up and keeping other people's money, give it to a homeless person. Recycle.

2 June *Eat only fresh foods.* Take the time today to prepare your meals with ingredients that do not start out in a package, can, jar, carton, or bottle. Find creative ways of cooking without oil and butter. This may sound difficult, and at first it might be, but by the end of the day you'll be an expert at preparing foods from their original state.

This of course means eating plenty of fresh fruits, vegetables, and grains. Be creative. If you like salsa, dice up a few tomatoes, add onions, cilantro, and some spices, and olé! Or make an elaborate fruit salad, with nuts and assorted seeds thrown in.

See what fresh food really looks like before you eat it. Smell the variety of aromas. Examine the different textures and shapes, the range of colors that food offers. Get input from friends or the members of your family. Ask them what fresh foods they'd like to eat, and prepare different dishes that incorporate them.

3 June *Dye an outfit or an article of clothing.* Tie-dyeing is a lot of fun, and something everyone in your family can do, but even if you're not that ambitious, you can select a single color that fits your mood.

Perhaps you have something that you've always loved to wear, something that has been almost like a close friend, but is now woefully out of style only because of its color. Dye it. Change the way it looks. You can create something entirely new just by buying dye in almost any store that sells notions, and following the package directions. Of course, some things are easier to dye than others, but with many items you'll discover that you didn't need to spend a lot of money on a new outfit. You've got something new almost by magic.

If you want to tie-dye a shirt, bunch up various surfaces of the material and hold them in place with rubber bands before dipping the shirt into the dye. Then repeat the process with different colors. Show your family and closest friends that you're willing to take risks, that you haven't lost your youthful panache. Look through a picture book of the Grateful Dead rock band for ideas. This activity will reconnect you with your youth without any loss of the wisdom you've gained over the years. You can have the best of both worlds.

4 June   *Throw stones in a pond.* Find a small, serene body of water, one that is accessible to you. On your way to the water, pick up any small stones or rocks that appear in your path. You might gather thirty or more, so that you'll feel like you really paid attention to the task, not skimmed the surface.

When you arrive at your destination, find a quiet spot, pick up your first stone, and throw it into the water. Watch the trajectory as it flies to its appointed destination. Did it end up closer or farther than you thought it would? Listen for the *plunk* as it meets the still water, and watch the splash and then the ripples as it disappears into the deep.

Make sure all your throws count. As you throw each stone, watch to see if it looks like the others, or if it has its own unique life in flight. If you prefer, skim a few flat stones, and watch them skip over the surface of the water before settling in. How many skips can you run up?

Discover the feeling of having nothing to do but throw stones in the water. Experience the languid, lazy feeling that accompanies the beginning of summer. As you throw each stone, think of something you like about your life, something to be thankful for.

5 June   *Go camping.* You don't have to make a big deal of this. A short trip in the car over the weekend will probably bring you closer to nature than you've been in a long time.

Pack up your car with the gear you'll need. You can probably borrow it from a friend if you don't have the basics. You can get away with a sleeping bag, tent, cooler, stove, and lantern or flashlight. You don't need anything else. Regardless of where you live, there are campgrounds within a few hours' drive.

Once you're among the trees, birds, stars, and the silence, set up camp and allow yourself to start to unwind. Slow down the pace. Find your spot in the wilderness. Take note of how delicious food tastes when you've cooked it yourself over a stove in the outdoors. Even a cheese sandwich or freeze-dried soup will take on a different flavor when you eat it away from your normal habitat.

Take your time with everything you do. Feel the slower, more deliberate rhythm of nature. Before you slide into your sleeping bag, look at the stars, and then quietly turn out your lantern and drift off into dream land.

When you awake, make a hot beverage to warm you up as the sun slowly makes its mark on the day.

6 June   *Clean out your refrigerator and food shelves.* Do for your food storage what you did for your clothes closets back in March. Go through every nook and cranny and throw out or give away what you know you're not going to eat.

Do you still have a few cases of pork and beans left over from your bachelor days? Give them to a food bank. Is there a half-eaten burrito tucked away among the artichokes you forgot to cook last month? Throw them all away, or gather up anything that could be used for composting.

When you finish, your food shelves and refrigerator should contain only items that you know you will eat. You might want to consolidate all your mustards, oils, and salad dressings to save space. Examine your freezer and see if there is anything there that you know you could do without. Throw it away. Forget the guilt. There's no guilt—your intentions were pure, but you know you never really did like leftovers. It's all right to acknowledge that fact by getting rid of anything that's been there far too long.

7 June   *Compose your own greeting card.* Father's Day is coming up. This is a perfect opportunity to put on paper what you've been wanting to tell your father, grandfather, son, brother, or husband. Or if there's a special birthday on the horizon, make time to think about the person you want to acknowledge and write your own card.

You can buy a blank card or, if you're feeling artistic, even design your own from scratch. You can try to mimic traditional greeting cards, but you can also develop your own style, or write a poem, or say just a few words that come from deep in your heart.

Pretend that commercial greeting cards do not exist, that it is your mission to write to this special person and no one else can do it. You have been chosen as designated writer. Make sure he or she can sense that you have thought deeply about your words before putting them on paper. Think of how delighted this person will be to hear directly from *you*.

8 June   *Trade outfits with someone.* Get in touch with a friend or relative and ask if he or she would like to swap a shirt or sweater or tie for a day. Do this at a time when you'll be noticed, when people will see that you've got on something you've never worn before, something that's not even your style.

Select your swap mate on the basis of your appreciation of his or her taste, and see what it feels like to be wearing his or her clothes.

This is another example of how easy it is to incorporate new things into your life without spending money. Trading outfits allows you to enlarge your wardrobe simply and easily. It connects you with another person so that both of you benefit from your association. It takes you out of your everyday reality and allows you to experiment without much risk. If you like what your buddy lent you, you can trade for good, or buy a similar item or two, knowing it works for you. If you find you like the things you own better, try swapping with someone else.

9 June　*Plan a party.* Sit down, think about what you'd like to celebrate, and start jotting down ideas. Is someone in your house graduating? Getting married? Or do you feel you'd like to have all your friends and acquaintances in one place at one time, that it's time you stopped telling Fred about Marge, that they finally met?

Make up a guest list. Put down everyone you think you'd like to invite. You can always pare down later. Write a list of people who might want to help you. Think of the best place to have this party. What kind of food do you want? What type of atmosphere suits you? Will your party have a theme? Discuss the event with at least one other person. Exchange ideas. Think about the parties you have attended that really impressed you. Was it the food? The hospitality? The guests? The occasion?

Try to do as much as possible beforehand so you can be relaxed for the gathering. Plan for a 75 percent turnout of the people who say they'll attend, and try not to be disappointed if people you want to be there aren't. Everyone who is meant to attend will show up.

On the day of the party, be cool and calm and keep thinking about how successful your party will be. Imagine the guests arriving, and the festivities building as the evening wears on, and everyone remarking to you what a great party it is. Ask some people ahead of time if they'd help clean up, offering to give them care packages of leftovers. (By tomorrow, you probably won't want to look at the food again.)

Make sure someone takes pictures.

10 June   *Take a mental health day.* This seems similar to playing hooky from work, which you did in January, but it's different. Pretend you're sick. Spend the day as if you were ten years old and staying home from school. Stay in pajamas and lounge in bed all day, surrounded by magazines, watching television, taking naps, and letting the world go by without you.

Don't answer the phone. Make tea, and get in touch with what it was like to be in grammar school, when staying home was a treat that was probably given to you once in a while.

Make time for yourself today. Let everything take as long as it needs to. Remember, you're really under the weather.

Whether your symptoms are physical or mental makes no difference. You can't afford to push yourself, or your condition might worsen. Keep in mind that your sole objective is to get well, even if all you need is a day to recover from the stresses of daily life.

11 June   *Plan an adventure.* Think of the people with whom you'd like to spend this adventure, call them, arrange a date and time to discuss some possibilities, and then start thinking about what you might want to do

Your adventure might be as modest as a walk across town, or as grand as a river-rafting trip. Whatever you decide to do, make sure you see it as a real adventure. It qualifies as an adventure if it's something out of the ordinary; something you've always wanted to do; something you never thought you could do; or something that other people think you should—or shouldn't—do.

When you begin your adventure, try not to think about the destination, but rather focus on what you're doing for its own sake. As Robert Louis Stevenson said, "To travel hopefully is a better thing than to arrive." If you're walking in an unfamiliar part of town, pay special attention to the scenery, the architecture, the ambience of the area. If you have chosen river rafting, bear in mind that each moment along the way contains the seed of a joyful experience. Each point in time can provide all the excitement you could ever want. The "trip" is merely the sum total of every individual moment you experience. As you move along the river, recognize both the power and the serenity, the way the water carries you along as it also holds you up.

When your adventure is over, it will now be part of your life experience, what you're comfortable with, what you know you can do. The next time you plan an adventure, try to make it even more daring. River rafting can become rock climbing, and a walk across town can become a walk across a strange town. Babysitting for one child can turn into babysitting for two, or even a decision to start a family of your own, one of the biggest adventures of all.

12 June   *Forget about diets.* Stop the process of denying your system what it requires and start to accept your shape. If you feel yourself wanting to shed a few pounds, imagine yourself at that ideal weight and allow your appetite to adjust itself gradually, so you eat what you need, in the amounts that allow you to feel satisfied but not too full.

Starving yourself only gives your system the wrong signal. It sends the message that your body needs to conserve what it has in order to live, a natural condition in times of deprivation. When you return to eating normally, your body reacts to the increase in food by overstoring it, holding on to it for the next time it doesn't have enough.

Extreme diets generally don't work. In fact, they are more likely to produce the opposite result. If you want to attain your ideal weight, exercise at least three times per week, and eat only when you're hungry.

Eat slowly so that you can stop when you're truly full, instead of eating extra food between the time you've had enough and the time your body recognizes that fact. Trust your instincts as far as what your body really wants by imagining how you will feel after you eat what you're craving, and eat only what truly satisfies you. The more you eat nutritional food, the more your body will ask for it.

13 June   *Do something without your clothes on.* Skinny-dipping is one obvious option. Get yourself invited to the house of a friend who has a hot tub or pool, or go out into the country and find a secluded pond in which you can swim without being disturbed. Or visit a nude beach.

One way of reconnecting with life as it was when you were first born is to be naked. Clean your house or apartment in the nude. Or if you can't commit to something quite this unusual, just clean one room! Go about your business as if there was nothing especially different about what you're doing, except that your clothes are somewhere other than on your body.

Any daily activity can be temporarily enhanced by performing it in the altogether. Doing this is a great way of discovering the part of you that is open to adventure, to wackiness, and to discovering the pleasures of your body. If you have the nerve to do it, do whatever you're doing in front of a mirror. Appreciate the way your body looks.

14 June, Flag Day *Think about what the United States means to you.* Look at this country with an even eye. Give it credit for what it provides, and don't overlook what it withholds.

What is Flag Day? Why did Congress enact legislation to commemorate the adoption of Betsy Ross's initial design by the Continental Congress?

What were the political and economic principles for which men and women fought during the Revolution? Who were Washington, Jefferson, Franklin, and Adams? What were their priorities? What did concepts like freedom, liberty, equality, representation, separation ofpowers, and civil rights mean to them? What motivated them to put their lives on the line for these principles?

How close are we today to the ideals set forth in the Declaration of Independence, the Constitution, and the Bill of Rights? What has changed about America in the past two hundred years? What has stayed the same? What were the issues that dominated that time? What questions plague us now?

Let your representatives in Congress know how you feel about the current state of affairs. Write a letter to your senators and representative. Tell them what you think the most pressing problems are and ask them to let you know what progress is being made to solve them.

15 June *Hire a student to do a summer job.* If you have a business, see if a high school or college student can help out. It could be part-time or full-time, depending on your needs. Hiring a student for the summer gives him or her the opportunity to work, to earn money, and to build self-esteem.

Even if you don't have a business, you have the opportunity to hire a student during the summer months. It could be on a project basis, or perhaps several days each week.

Babysitting is a perfect reason to employ a student, but there are other tasks that usually merit help as well. Washing your car, cleaning out your garage, running errands, or even painting your house can all be done by teenagers.

Make sure you set out the terms of your agreement with him or her at the outset. Clear agreement on hourly rates and expectations of promptness, direct communication, and quality of work can set the tone for a mutually beneficial relationship.

Providing a positive work experience for a young person may set him or her off in the right direction for life. And you can also give this student a recommendation that will open doors for him or her for a long time.

16 June   *Watch the full moon rise at sunset.* In fact, that's the only time you can watch it, since it's a unique peculiarity of the heavens that the full moon always rises at this time.

There's a full moon every month, so if you miss it or the weather is overcast, look for the next one. Find a comfortable spot where you can sit for a while. Face east, and make sure you arrive before the moon is scheduled to rise. Bring a camera if you'd like.

Keep your eyes focused on the horizon, to a spot where you think the moon will come up. When it first rises, the moon will appear uncommonly big, as if it has puffed itself up for the performance. You won't be able to see it actually move, but before long it will have cleared the horizon and appear to be perched upon the earth.

The sky will darken as the moon continues its ascent. Notice how the colors on the surface of the earth change as the sun sinks deeper into the opposite horizon. Before long, the moon will appear to have regained its normal shape. In about an hour, as it slowly makes its way across the sky, the moon will not look like the same heavenly body you watched appear before you.

17 June   *Fight fair.* If you have an argument or dispute with someone, make sure you stick to the issue. Express the thoughts or feelings that pertain to what's in front of you. And try not to let your mood affect your reaction to what people are doing in your presence. Don't hit someone with a barrage just because you feel bad and he or she is in the line of fire.

When you argue, try to detach the person from the position. Don't make disparaging references to his or her character, intentions, or alleged motivations. Stick to how you feel. Keep the focus on your position. Rather than saying what you think the other person is doing, tell him or her what it feels like to you.

Avoid using "always" or "never." Obviously, you are trying to make your case, but overstating it takes away from both the immediacy of the issue and the strong feelings of the moment. It's much easier to be heard if you concentrate on being accurate.

Remember to deal with the "truth" of the matter, rather than merely the facts. The truth will get you closer to resolution. Listen carefully to the other person's position. Many times the problem arises out of frustration at not being heard. Listen and speak from your heart. What are you really angry about?

Make it a point not to go to bed angry. Even if your dispute is with someone with whom you do not live, agree to continue the discussion at another time rather than storm off in a huff. Resolution does not have to take place immediately. But insist that it's your intention that each of your positions will eventually be aired and the dispute resolved.

18 June   *Work before 9 A.M. and after 5 P.M., and take off in between.* You can easily do a full day's work and still have the entire day free. You can even do more than eight hours if you're so inclined.

Get up early and start working by 6 A.M. You can work in a comfortable spot at home or in a quiet public place like a café or a library—if one is open this early. While it might be difficult to make business calls, you certainly could write reports, read important articles or memos that you've been putting off, or just contemplate your work from a broader perspective.

At 9 A.M., stop. Just get up, put your work papers away, and enjoy your freedom. You've already worked 37.5 percent of your day, so see this as your lunch hour. You can spend your time in any way you choose. Go to the beach. Read an absorbing novel. Have a midday fling with your spouse.

At 5 P.M. resume your work. You'll be fresh and alert, and since some time has passed since you last worked, it will feel like a new day. If you live on the East Coast you can make calls to the West Coast. Or you can continue on what you started in the morning. If you can arrange it, have a meeting or two this evening. People may be delighted to share in the uniqueness of your approach to your job.

19 June *Take a break from a daily habit.* The simplest change can make a big difference in the way you see life. If you smoke, give it up for a day. If you eat too much junk food, read or take a walk instead; every time you feel yourself reaching for the bag, walk out and smell the freshness of the air. If you crack your knuckles, stretch your fingers.

Even if your habit is a healthy one, refrain from doing it today. If you usually run five miles a day, sit still. If your breakfast consists of nonfat yogurt and berries, have a *cafèlatte* and a chocolate croissant. If you go to work and immediately start discussing with co-workers how bad things are, how stupid management is, and how you would run the company differently, quietly excuse yourself from the coffee machine cut-up session and read a travel article instead.

Whenever you feel the urge to engage in your habit merely because it's a habit, stop yourself and do something else. Think about what you're going to do ahead of time. Have a plan. Have alternatives. Be creative. Instead of tippling two drinks when you get home from work, do a crossword puzzle over a glass of carrot juice.

20 June   *Collaborate with a child on a project.*
It could be anything, but chances are you'll do better if the activity is related to the child's life, not yours. Writing a story together is something that can provide incalculable pleasure.

First, talk about the story. Discuss the characters, the setting, the place and time that are most appealing to each of you. When you have the details in mind, move on to the message. What important lesson about life do you and the child want to convey in the story?

Make sure you illustrate the book. Your colleague can draw the trees, the house, and the white picket fence while you draw Mommy, Daddy, and Spot. Write the text together. Go over the story to make sure it makes sense to both of you, then bind it and give it a title.

Or you can write a song. Ask the child what his or her favorite subject is and compose a few bars and lyrics to celebrate it.

Notice if you feel yourself wanting to control the process. If so, pull back. Let the child take the lead.

21 June   *Ask for a refund.* Is there something you've purchased recently that you've had second thoughts

about, that isn't what you really want, that perhaps you were talked into by an overeager salesperson who had his interest in mind and not yours? Take it back. You don't need to keep it.

Even if the established policy of the store is to give no refunds, ask for one anyway. Today's suggestion is a mini-course in assertiveness training. Whether you get your money back or not is irrelevant; what's important is that you challenge the rules, that you go beyond the given.

Acknowledge the store's policy and make your case. If they ask for a reason, tell them that on second thought you don't want what you've purchased, that you have no need for it, that you were just browsing and acted on impulse, that it doesn't fit, that it's the wrong color, that you changed your mind. Persist. Tell the people that you'd appreciate your money back and that you'll let all your friends and acquaintances know how accommodating the store is, how easy it is to deal with, how understanding, cooperative, polite, and service oriented.

If they balk, tell the store that if they return your money they'll have a customer for life, that you intend to spend the amount of the refund many times over, and that your friends will do that as well.

If they do not budge, politely but firmly tell them that they're being penny-wise and pound-foolish and that they are missing a chance to think long-term. If you succeed, think about the process you've just undergone and realize that you are not wedded to your decisions.

22 June   *Read a different newspaper.* If you always read a local paper, read a national one. If you limit yourself to national newspapers, read an international one. There is a variety from which to choose, and each one is a world unto itself.

Actually, there is no such thing as news; it's all a point of view. If you always read the same paper, recognize that your point of view of events is influenced by that of the newspaper. Reading a different paper will introduce you to a different point of view.

This is not just the case with the editorial page; point of view permeates the entire endeavor. A newspaper constantly makes choices as to what stories it wants to cover, how much emphasis it will devote to which topics, and where it will feature local, national, and international pieces, to name just a few considerations.

Go through the entire newspaper, and see what is different from the paper you normally read. You might want to compare coverage with your everyday paper's. See if a particular story reads the same way in both papers, or whether it's hard to tell if you're even reading about the same event.

23 June   *Tell someone the story of your life.* It could be the person closest to you, even if he or she has heard a lot of it over the time you've been together, or a total stranger. Pick someone with whom you feel comfortable and who would like to know all about you.

Agree before you begin on how much time you will allow yourself. Since you're obviously going to have a time limit, you will have to pick out the experiences that have shaped you, determined you, made you uniquely who you are.

There are many areas that merit attention. What about your childhood? What about school? When did you start to get involved in matters of the heart? What were your first serious life choices? When did you make them, and of what did they consist?

Who were the people who influenced you most? What serendipitous forces interceded in your life to change it forever? Are you the person you thought you'd become? Are you fulfilling your dreams?

Whether you survived the Holocaust, were the first American to buy a transistor radio, or spent far too many years in an insurance office checking documents, it is a rare and precious gift both to yourself and to others to share your life story.

When you've finished, ask the person who listened to you to do the same. And then talk about how different or alike your lives are.

24 June   *Hold hands with someone special.* It could be your grandmother, a favorite uncle, a lover or best friend, your husband, wife, or child. One of the ways to get

the most out of this interaction is to take a walk with the person with whom you want to be close.

Holding hands connects you in a small, but significant, way. You are together, yet most of your body remains free to move at its own pace. In other cultures, people routinely touch each other in public. It is not unusual to see people strolling arm in arm, talking animatedly, or enlarging the potential of the moment through frequent touching.

When you gently touch someone in an innocuous way, you affirm your love and regard for them, and their similar feelings for you. It allows you to be more intimate, more relaxed in the presence of others, and reduces the thickness of the armor that separates us from other people.

25 June   *Research something.* It doesn't have to be something significant, or something you need to know. It can be a topic you've simply wondered about and never took the time to investigate.

Let's say you've wanted to learn about the mating habits of the bald eagle. You could read books or articles on ornithology or visit this bird's habitat and watch its movements personally. You could go to the library, find out who the acknowledged experts are, and call or write to them.

You may even become something of an expert yourself. You may find—over time and with considerable effort—that your own observations, evidence, and data contradict the accepted explanations or interpretations and that you have an original contribution to make to the field.

Often the impetus to expand your knowledge results from extreme personal circumstances. Maybe your father needs to have open-heart surgery and you want to know more about the risks. Call people. Ask questions. Find out all you can. At some point, at some depth, you'll find that specialized knowledge goes beyond its own particular category and partakes of universal knowledge.

26 June *Pick berries.* This is a splendid way to pass a morning or afternoon, experience firsthand what farm life is like, spend time with your family or friends, and come away with something delicious to eat.

Regardless of where you live, there are berry farms nearby. Strawberries, raspberries, blackberries, and blueberries are all within reach. Just drive out to the farm, ask for a bucket or box, get whatever minimal instructions are needed, and start picking.

With strawberries, you will be assigned to a row. You can pick berries on either side of the row. It will probably outlast you, but you can, spending an hour or two, pick several pounds of berries.

When you get home you can eat them raw or make jam or preserves, strawberry shortcake, or wine. You'll feel closer to the earth, to the source of all life, and have delicious fun in the process.

27 June   *Carry an amulet with you.* Pick something small and dear to you, something that has special significance. It could be a ring, a charm, a coin, someone's picture or lock of hair. As long as you associate good times or warm feelings with this item or the person connected to it, it qualifies.

Imagine that your amulet is now your good-luck charm as you carry it around with you. You can put it in your pocket, wear it on a chain around your neck, or keep it in your purse or briefcase with your papers. Keep reminding yourself that it's there. Convince yourself that you're going to have good luck all day because of your amulet, that it will attract the things you want and ward off things and people that are not right for you.

At night, before you go to bed, thank your amulet for the fine work it did keeping you safe and fortunate all day.

28 June   *Think about your "giants."* Giants are people who have had the greatest impact on your life, who came along at a time when you needed to hear or experience something and told you about or led you to exactly what it was.

Each middle-aged or mature life usually has about four or five giants. If there are significantly fewer than that, you may not be acknowledging how others have influenced you.

In that case, try to think back to times when you know you changed. Who was in your life then? How did you form your views? Who influenced you?

Now consider whether you have transcended your giants, if you have gone beyond what you learned from them to forge a way of life that is completely and uniquely your own. See if you can actually imagine yourself disagreeing with one of your giants, even though at a certain point in your life you hung on every word he or she uttered.

Make finding new giants that are appropriate at this point in your life a goal.

29 June   *Join an organization.* It can be local, or the local branch of a national organization; it can be related to school, career, or a lifelong interest. Or your interest could be fueled simply by curiosity.

Joining an organization may or may not put you in touch with like-minded people. You may find it inconceivable that so many people could think as you do, or you may discover— because an issue is so complex—that your interest in or opinion on a subject is radically different from those who profess to share your views.

Ask questions about how the organization is structured. How much are dues (if any), and to what do these fees entitle you? What is the mission of the organization? What is its history? Talk to some of the other members and get their impressions of the solidity of the organization.

Think about how much time you can devote to the group. Is it something in which you want to take an active role, serving on committees, making phone calls, running for office, or do you merely want to be informed of activities, events, and current information on recent developments that pertain to the organization?

The association is what counts, not the level of involvement. Joining a group is a step in defining who you are.

30 June   *Get wet.* Visit a private or public pool, a lake, the ocean, a river or stream, and spend some time splashing around or swimming.

Note how refreshing the water feels, cooling your body as it revitalizes your spirit. When you emerge from the water, put on lotion and let the sun slowly dry your skin, feeling the warmth return to your body in the heightened intensity of summer.

When you feel hot again, jump back in. Do this as many times as your day permits.

The Importance of Breathing

Mindfulness is a subtle concept. It is difficult to define because it is essentially a paradox. The idea is to employ your mind to immerse yourself in something so deeply that you go beyond your mind—it literally falls away—and find yourself in an even deeper part of your being, for which there is really no word in English, although soul or spirit or the unconscious comes close.

Another name for this process is meditation. Your form of meditation can consist of anything, from baseball to baking, selling to silent sitting, and, like any other skill, it improves with practice. But if you want to focus your practice on the basics, concentrate on your breathing.

Very few people pay enough attention to their breathing, taking it—like many other things in their life—for granted. Breathing is both a literal requirement and figurative symbol of life, of renewal, of rebirth. Every time we fill our lungs we are, in a sense, born again. Breathing is also a metaphor for the fresh material required by both our physical bodies and social selves.

Happiness—one very real consequence of mindful action—has a physical component, and it is connected to our breathing. Why is it that times of fear and anxiety can shorten our breath? What takes place in our circulatory systems that restricts our ability to take in that which we need to live? Is it mere coincidence that the times we are farthest from happiness are the times we cannot fully breathe?

Happiness is a fundamentally human trait, and if you want to enlarge your sphere of happiness, pay attention to your breathing. If you could start out by becoming aware of how you breathe, what your inhale feels like, then what your exhale feels like, for just a few minutes a day, that awareness will have created a different life for you. You will have gotten that much closer to the source of all pleasure and pain—your own body. A life's worth of sensual exploration will have begun.

Good, deep breathing produces clarity, and clarity of mind, of spirit, of purpose, can form the foundation of your health. So many things can rest upon it, good things, happy moments, a self-created life. Good, deep breathing enables you to absorb the whole, indiscriminately capturing the essential life force of every moment.

⚇ July ⚇

1 July, Canada Day   *Start a conversation with your neighbor.* Make sure you do this with someone you've never really talked to before. If you regularly speak with your two next-door neighbors, go to the house on the other side of your next-door neighbor and start by commenting on their beautiful garden, their adorable kids, or the deck they just put in.

If you live in an apartment building, knock on the door of the next apartment, introduce yourself formally, and strike up a conversation. Talk about what's going on in your neighborhood, your city, or, if you feel you can be more personal, your life. Ask your neighbor where he or she lived before, and trade tips on where to get the best deals on light bulbs or cereal.

Invite him or her to your house or apartment for a cup of coffee or lemonade. Try to break through the barriers to friendship with the people who live closest to you. If you are in an isolated area, walk or ride to the nearest house, introduce yourself, and be as warm and friendly as you can possibly be.

Take the initiative. Don't wait for your neighbor to be neighborly. Show him or her how it's done.

2 July   *Organize a household meeting.* Check with the members of your immediate family, or your roommates, pick a date and hour that is convenient for everyone, and set aside a certain amount of time to discuss the issues that affect all of you.

Appoint one person to be in charge of the agenda and make sure he or she solicits everyone for suggestions. Distribute the agenda at least one day before the meeting. The items to be discussed don't have to be major; they only need to merit household-wide attention.

At the beginning of the meeting, select one person as the chair and give him or her the mandate to keep the discussion focused on a particular topic, to gently but firmly balance everyone's need to be heard with the need to keep the issues in view and all the topics covered. It's a good idea to call on the least vociferous family members first and provide them with the opportunity to speak so they won't be unduly influenced by the most opinionated.

Make sure everyone is heard and can speak freely. Don't interrupt the speaker. It is the chair's responsibility to watch for unnecessary repetition. If there is consensus on actions that are to be taken, make sure each family member is clear about the nature and time frame of his or her assignment.

The point of the meeting is to discuss concerns that affect family life in a manner that encourages openness and candor. If the first meeting is stiff and people don't know what to say, keep trying.

If you live alone, gather a group of friends with whom you feel close and hold a friends meeting.

3 July   *Be an optimist.* Regardless of what others say, look at the bright side of everything. Have faith that

everything will turn out fine, for you personally, for other people, and for the world in general.

Don't let this belief falter. Act out of your unwavering faith. If others say you are being unduly optimistic, tell them that it is impossible to be overly optimistic, that every experience—even an unpleasant one—carries with it the seed of something fruitful.

How does it feel to expect only good things to happen? Foreign? Familiar? Impossible? Easy? How do others react when you put a positive spin on everything? Do they think you've gone off the deep end, or note with admiration the change in your attitude? Count how many times you're told you're being unrealistic, and then mention Henry Ford and the Wright brothers.

If you are already an optimistic person, turn it up a notch. See if you can get close to being a ten on a scale of one to ten.

4 July, Independence Day *Memorize the first paragraph of the Declaration of Independence.* Ask a family member or friend to do this with you. It's not very long. It begins this way: "When in the course of human events, it becomes necessary for one people to dissolve the political bands which have connected them with another . . ."

Talk about what independence means to you with the person who's sharing in the memorization. Write down your respective thoughts and express them. Save what you write. Do this each year on Independence Day and see how your notions of liberty change from year to year.

5 July   *Look through a book on another country.* Think about a country that has always fascinated you, or that you've always wanted to visit, or perhaps that you know nothing about, and get a book that shows both the land and people of that country in their splendor.

Try to get a book that has color photos. A little bit about the history and development of the country would add an immense amount of information to your understanding. See if the presentation of the country in the book jibes with your preconceived notions, even if you know the country well and have visited it many times. Are there things you can still learn about this place?

Select a book that talks about the regional differences within the country, regardless of its size. You might want to choose a volume that talks about the language and provides some examples of common expressions and greetings.

It doesn't matter how well known or obscure your country is. What do you know about Botswana? Do you know the official language, or when it was granted independence? The important thing is to act as if you are actually in the country itself by immersing yourself in a pictorial representation of it. You'll get a feel for the place without having to be there.

6 July   *Have a sing-along.* Get a group of people together, outdoors if possible, and make sure one of your group plays an instrument. A guitar, piano, or harmonica is probably best. A violin might not work as well.

The one who plays the instrument will probably get to choose most of the songs, but it's important that everyone join in. Stick to the songs that everyone knows. Folk songs and popular songs are usually the most familiar—"If I Had a Hammer" and Beatles tunes are always favorites—but if your musician can perform show tunes or even Gregorian chants, then give them a try. You can even rent a *karaoke* machine to provide actual background music.

Don't worry about singing on-key. The louder the singing, the less troublesome off-key voices become. Give anyone who requests it the opportunity to sing solo. Encourage duets. Make this a real participatory event. Assure people that their talents are not being judged, and that the point of this exercise is just plain fun.

If your group really gets going on this, you can sing for hours. Time stops. You'll enter into a kind of reverie that is all too rare these days.

7 July   *Make an introduction.* Fix someone up, as we used to say. Think about an unattached person you know, someone who would like to be with his or her true partner. Now think about someone who you feel might meet those qualifications.

Ask your friend if he's interested in being introduced to someone you think he might like. Tell him it doesn't have to be a big deal, that you think you know someone he'd like to meet.

Ask your friend or acquaintance to be open and receptive to your suggested introduction, to suspend his stereotypes and prejudgments and really look at this person carefully. Ask him to look at this woman's inner qualities rather than her superficial characteristics. Ask him to see how it feels to be with her rather than what she looks like, or whether her hair is the right color.

Making introductions for the purposes of love provides incredible joy if it works, and only practice will improve your skills. Follow your intuition. You never know when people are going to like each other.

8 July   *Say "yes" when you mean "yes" and "no" when you mean "no."* Resist every temptation to compromise your desires in any way. If someone asks you to do something, and his power of persuasion is good, examine your inner feelings to see if you want to do it or if you're being coerced.

If you feel you don't really want to comply but would be saying "yes" because of peer or societal pressure, say "no."

Don't do it. The ability to say no is an important step along the road to the full enjoyment of life.

Similarly, say "yes" when you mean "yes." If you want to do something, accept the offer or suggestion with enthusiasm and clarity. Forget about what others may say. Be your own guide. Play the game by the rules you set up. Learning to say yes is just as important to your development as a person as your ability to say no.

If you're not sure of your feelings when someone asks you to do something, say "maybe," and then tell him or her you'll follow up when you're more certain.

9 July *Relate food to your mood.* Are you feeling the need to nurture yourself? Make a hot cup of tea and a bowl of mushy oatmeal. Do you feel sexy and loving? Open a bottle of champagne, indulge in a delicious piece of chocolate, and place yourself in a luxurious environment.

Do you need to break loose, to be more feisty? Eat as much spicy Asian food as you can tolerate. Are you feeling restless? Chomp on a carrot or celery stick, or eat a few pretzels. The action of your jaw will focus and release energy. If you're feeling that you want to be grounded, make yourself a bowl of vegetable soup, or a plate of beans and rice.

Do you want to get hold of something? Sink your teeth into a triple-decker hero, hoagie, or submarine. Do you want to lighten up? Eat a salad.

Matching your mood with the appropriate food demonstrates to yourself how much of what you eat is tied to what you feel, and vice versa.

10 July   *Get in motion.* Do something that lets you experience the thrill of movement. Find a body of water and get on skis. Go to an amusement park and ride on the roller coaster, or, if your stomach can't take that much excitement, on the Ferris wheel.

Jump up and down on a trampoline. Go sailing, or hop a ride in a hot-air balloon.

Feel the power of the wind as it rushes by you. Feel the exhilaration as you find yourself more in sync with the spinning of the earth than you normally are. Feel gravity work its best to push you back.

If you have the skills, the training, and the experience, try hang gliding, windsurfing, or riding a motorcycle. Take all precautions, follow all directions, and feel the thrill of each moment.

11 July   *Make plans to visit old friends.* Call up someone about whom you've been thinking and ask if you can stay with him or her for a few days. Plan to stay no more

than three. Actually, two nights will suffice, lest you run the risk of realizing Benjamin Franklin's proverb about guests and fish—after three days they both stink.

When you arrive, let things unfold naturally. Try not to rush to re-create old times. Let the intimacy that is or once was rekindle itself. Be where your hosts are. Go with their rhythm. If they want to talk about old times, join them. If they want to know about you, tell them what's been going on. If they'd rather talk about themselves, listen carefully.

Offer to take them out to dinner the next night. Show your appreciation of their friendship and the sharing of their home. Buy them something small as a token of your gratitude for their hospitality.

If the time spent with these friends went well, invite them to visit you at some point in the future. If the visit was less than what you expected, thank them for the weekend and think about other people you might want to visit sometime.

12 July *Play horseshoes.* You can go to a park, or set up the stakes in your backyard if you have one. The game of horseshoes teaches you how to concentrate and perform repeated action, is easy to learn, and encourages friendly competition and good cheer.

The way to really enjoy this game is to play with people of all ages. Kids and grandparents can have just as much fun as adults, maybe even more.

Another great thing about horseshoes is that it flies in the face of convention by teaching the concept that almost *does* count, that even though the object is to get a ringer, getting closer to the stake than your opponent is good enough. You don't have to score every time to be good at this game. Just keep pitching horseshoes and your share of ringers will come to you eventually.

13 July *Have a tea party.* It can be an intimate affair with a special friend, an event with six or eight of the people you routinely see, or, if there is no one in your life right now with whom you'd like to share this special occasion, yourself.

First, get out your china or your best dishes. No paper plates or plastic cups. Make this little event something special. Steep a pot of tea and serve it with milk, sugar, honey, or lemon. Have some small pastries on hand to sweeten the afternoon.

Is the tenor of the gathering different when you serve tea instead of coffee? Do you find the group discussing different things? Are people more polite, or are they much the same as they normally are?

Watch how the conversation progresses. Does one person dominate? Or does everyone join in? Do people say mostly negative or positive things? Are they generally optimistic or pessimistic? Do they talk mostly about themselves? Others? Do they discuss ideas?

When your tea party is over, ask if anyone volunteers to be the next host, and make it a regular feature of your social life.

14 July, Bastille Day *Do everything French.* Start the day with a croissant and a café au lait. Wear clothes that show the *tricolore—bleu, blanc, et rouge.* Go through the whole day speaking of *liberté, fraternité, et égalité.*

If you are a woman, wear something French underneath, or Chanel No. 5. If you are a man, wear a beret and ride your bicycle to work. Sing the opening lines of the *Marseillaise:* *"Allons enfants de la patrie, le jour de gloire est arrivé."*

In the evening, eat escargot or *foie gras,* and, if you're so inclined, end the day with a long, slow French kiss.

15 July *Consider alternative forms of healing.* The next time you experience symptoms of distress, see if the malady might be healed through methods outside mainstream circles.

For chronic symptoms, like aches in joints or the back, allergies, stomach problems, or a persistent cough, consult a practitioner who can administer acupuncture, homeopathic remedies, chiropractic techniques, herbal teas, and physical therapy such as Rolfing, Feldenkrais, the Heller method, and deep massage.

Investigate alternative medical practitioners as you would any physician. Explain your symptoms and ask if he or she could help you. Interview the practitioner. Get a feel not only for what he or she does, but for who he or she is. Ask about his background. See how you feel in her presence.

Sometimes alternative practices take longer to work. They join forces with the body's natural healing mechanisms. Ask your practitioner how long you should wait before judging the results.

16 July *Rearrange your furniture.* If you're feeling ambitious, you can take on your whole house or apartment. If you want to start out small, consider one room and work on that for a while.

You can either make an elaborate plan for your new room or be completely spontaneous. Start by moving the smallest, lightest piece you can find. See how that works. If you like how it looks, move another piece. Move one chair, one lamp, one bed, one couch at a time, and you will soon have a new room.

When you have created your new environment, sit or spend time in it for a while and see how it feels. Make minor changes if they're needed, or go through the whole process again. Have your room look exactly the way you want it to. Make this a continuous process, something you work on until it's just right.

17 July   *Sit in the dark.* Find a comfortable, quiet spot in which to take in the sounds of silence. You can be indoors or outdoors. What matters is that there is no light except for starlight or moonlight.

What does silence sound like? Is it really quiet? Or does it speak? If it does, does it speak loudly or softly? If you are outdoors and in nature, are you aware of summer sounds, of crickets and frogs and the sound of heat? If you are indoors, does the room speak to you? Does it have a symphony all its own that plays only in darkness? Is there a connection between the darkness in which you have immersed yourself and silence?

What does it feel like to be alone in the dark? Is it frightening, or comforting? Does it evoke memories of childhood? Does it take getting used to? Is it something you could see yourself doing often?

For a completely different experience, the next time the urge to sit in the dark engages you, do it wearing headphones playing your favorite music. See how that feels.

18 July   *Be different.* Do the opposite of everyone else. If everyone in your office goes to Moe's Diner on Tuesdays for lunch, suggest the group go to a different place

on Tuesday, or to Moe's on Wednesday. If you can't get them to agree to follow you, go alone. Start a new trend.

I once had a drink with a friendly group of men in a small bar on a Sunday evening in Basel, Switzerland. One of the members casually mentioned that he had been coming to the same bar every Sunday night for the past twenty-seven years. It seemed to me it was time for a change.

Get off cruise control. Shake up your life. If everyone in your office wears suspenders, wear a belt.

My fifth-grade teacher used to trot out a story to illustrate how those who don't conform are oblivious to their own behavior. At a dance, a mother was observing her daughter, who couldn't follow the rest of the crowd. At last the mother exclaimed, "Oh, my, everybody's out of step but my Katie."

Be like Katie. Be completely oblivious to what everyone else is doing. If only I had known that as a ten-year-old . . .

19 July   *Take your sense of romance to the next highest level.* If you've never danced the tango before, do it today. If you never wear cologne, start now. Make sure you feel a heightened awareness of romance, whether your attention is directed toward your wife, husband, partner, special friend, or yourself.

Today is the day to buy that first pair of black-silk boxer shorts, to have champagne with dinner, to reach new levels of decadence. Think about the nature of intimacy. What does it mean to you? Is it something you value? Does your life have enough of it? Are you more concerned with being loved than with loving?

If you feel the same way about yourself tomorrow as you do today, you didn't go far enough. Try again soon.

20 July ⁢ *Go to a matinee.* Experience the unfamiliarity of going to the movies in an unfamiliar way. Instead of going to the seven o'clock show, or the eight o'clock show, take in the two o'clock show.

When you enter the theater, first feel the blast of cold air as a welcome relief from the heat. Notice how uncrowded, unhurried, and unusual everything looks and feels, regardless of how many times you've been to this particular theater. Buy popcorn and something to drink.

Pick exactly the seat that appeals to you. You'll probably get your first choice with no trouble at all. You can sit up close, in the back row, on the aisle, in the middle. You can spread out and feel certain that no one will have a conversation behind you.

When the movie ends, take note of how it feels to reenter the "real" world. Feel the heat, the bustle and movement of busy people going about their business, and smile at the thought that for two hours, on a hot summer afternoon, you left it all behind and entered an entirely different reality.

21 July *Think about all the people in your life right now who really mean something to you.* These are people to whom, if you knew you would be gone tomorrow, you would not want to miss saying good-bye. You feel as if your life was somehow shaped by them, that they influenced you, molded you, brought you joy or pleasure or challenge.

Make a list of these people. Write down their names and then think of one small thing you could do to demonstrate your feeling for them. If it's someone to whom you speak on a regular basis—like your wife—just casually put your arms around her and tell her how much you love her, how much she means to you, how enriched your life is because she's in it.

For some on your list, a small gift, sent from far away, will be the most appropriate response. For others, a short note or a phone call will do the job.

Acknowledging the people around you makes you feel good and also maximizes the possibility that there will be more good feeling and support in the years to come. It's like putting money in a savings account. It stays there, accumulating interest, and you can draw on it forever.

22 July *Trade places with a cat.* For as long a time as you can maintain this role, go about your business the way a cat does. Try to see the world the way a cat would.

First, comport yourself in a manner that implies mystery. Be there, but also give the impression that you are up to something, that you have made a decision on which you are about to act but haven't yet commenced and would never reveal in advance.

Take meticulous care of yourself. Make sure your skin and hair are as pampered and cared for as you possibly can make them. Be particular about your food, eating only when you want to. Have someone brush your hair, slowly and gently, with at least a hundred strokes.

Purr, moan, and sigh as often as you can without someone asking if you are all right. Then, at other times, rub up against people and get them to stroke you, or find a warm sunny spot and curl up and take a nap.

23 July *Make a new friend.* It could be someone you meet today, someone you know only vaguely, or someone you know in a different context, like a business associate, or a merchant whose establishment you patronize. Your relationship could be at any stage of development. You want to create the conditions in which it can blossom into a full friendship.

Building a friendship is not merely a matter of chance. One way to help make an acquaintanceship turn into something more is to pick the person carefully. Many friendships don't happen because it isn't the right time for one party. The other person has to want to make a new friend as well, or at least be open to it.

The next step is to declare your intentions. Let him or her know, either directly or indirectly, that you are eager to deepen your relationship. Some people will admire your candor and respond to you, while others will not. Declaring your intentions doesn't mean that the two of you drop everything and spend every waking moment together. It does mean that you both have the intention of creating this new phenomenon—a friendship.

What you do in detail to make this friendship happen is really irrelevant. Whether you decide to do your laundry together, take swimming lessons, or just talk more, you'll find the friendship deepening if you make a commitment and see that it is being reciprocated.

24 July *Build a sand castle.* Make your sand castle a model of the house in which you'd like to live. If you already live in that house, make a model of your house. This is a project for which you'll be able to get all the help you need from children. If you want to build a really elaborate structure, round up four or five pairs of young hands to assist. Or you might want to go it alone, carefully incorporating every inclination—however whimsical—into your ideal home.

Create a dream with your own hands. Let your imaginative energy flow. See what comes out. Make sure you have the right tools. A short, sharp instrument like a popsicle stick might do well for details and finish work.

If you're constructing your dream house, imagine yourself living in it. See if you can conjure up what it would feel like to to design, build, and live in this house. Where would the kitchen go? How many bedrooms would it have? Would you have a home office? A guest room? Would your house have a wraparound front porch, a deck, patio, backyard? You're the designer/builder. You can make it work any way you like.

25 July *Build a fire.* Make it an outdoor fire. Find a spot in which it's legal, gather together some people you like, and bring marshmallows to roast or a pot of water for hot drinks. You could do this at the beach or in the woods. The point of this activity is to start the fire from scratch.

Gather up leaves, twigs, sticks, and any other kindling you can find. If you know that the spot you have chosen doesn't have enough wood, bring it from home, or find it along the way.

Even if the evening is warm, your fire will add a glow to everything and everyone there. It will serve to draw everyone's attention toward a central point. You can tell stories, sing songs, lie on the ground and watch the stars move across the sky, or cuddle with a special person, your spouse, or your children.

Your fire can last as long as you want it to. Sleeping by the fire is another way to get close to the elements, to reenact a scene that has taken place an infinite number of times since the very beginning of humankind.

26 July *Start to keep your personal finances in order.* Open every bill or invoice the day it arrives. Put the bill back in the envelope, write down the date by which you have to send the check, and put it in a pile with the other bills, arranged chronologically.

Designate a specific time each week or month for paying the bills. You might want to do it once a week, once every two weeks, or once a month. But make sure you do it by the time you decide upon.

Some people like to wait until the very last day before paying a bill; others like to pay as soon as the bill arrives. Either way is fine, but strive for consistency.

Your personal finances can be a source of real pleasure in your life—orderly, organized, accurate, timely. If you are a little short one month, call your creditors, explain your situation, and indicate when and how much you intend to pay back each month. You'll be surprised at how willing most people are to give you slack if you only ask.

27 July *Frame a photo, poster, or picture.* Do it yourself. You'll probably be able to find a shop nearby that has all the tools and equipment. Just go in with what you want to frame, ask for help, and within minutes you'll be getting instruction on the fine art of picture frame assembly.

Frames fit any budget. There are ways of keeping the cost down—choices that involve mounting, matting, frame selection—and other ways of driving it up. You choose.

When you start to assemble the frame, you'll see how everything fits together, why one task must come before another. You'll soon differentiate between the tasks that need to be precise and the tasks that don't. Take your time. Ask a lot of questions if you need to. People who work in frame shops are used to handling them. If you need help, speak up.

When you complete your work of art, marvel at how an ordinary photograph has suddenly been transformed into something quite spectacular through your intervention. See how satisfying craft work is, how rigorous discipline can sometimes lead to creativity.

28 July   *Go through your personal telephone book and conjure up a recollection of each person.* The longer you've had the book, the more fun, challenging, and stimulating the project. First, see if you can even remember everyone.

As your eyes fall on each name, address, and phone number, let this factual information evoke a feeling, a mood, of that particular time and place. Do you remember Sarah

Swanson, who left you waiting in the lobby as she called a client between the second and third acts of *La Traviata?*

Or is it Benjamin Bradford who comes to mind? He was the guy who sent telegrams to your office for a week after your first date—and you never even saw him again.

Your life is rich, varied, and probably includes many forgotten characters who made a small impact, but an impact nevertheless.

29 July   *Take a walk around your neighborhood.* Visit with the familiar, but try to see it for the first time, as if you've never seen it before. If you live in a city that has lots of sights, just cover four or five blocks. If your area is more spread out, you can cover more ground. If your habitat is rural, walk over meadows and down lovely lanes.

As you walk, take note of how much is new to you, how much you've never seen before, what you previously failed to notice even though you've passed by countless times. Is there a step or a doorway that has unusual markings? Is there a tree with a particularly majestic set of branches, or a fence that is perfectly nestled into the hillside? Keep in mind the things that strike you as fresh or peculiar.

We often take the familiar for granted. We fail to see how varied it is, how satisfying and fulfilling and surprising it can be. Anytime you feel yourself taking some aspect of your life for granted, just take a jaunt around familiar sites and see them through fresh eyes.

30 July *Keep fresh flowers nearby.* Your desk at work is a perfect place to demonstrate your intention to honor beauty. You don't have to have a full bouquet. A single rose will do.

Having fresh flowers on hand allows your senses to be stimulated in almost every way. The scent will remind you constantly that you are in the presence of something extraordinary. You can look up at any time to gaze at one of the most perfect forms nature has to offer, replete with vibrant color and unique shape. You can even press your finger against a thorn, ever so lightly, just to be reminded of the protection that the rose needs to keep away unwanted advances.

Do the flowers alter your mood? Do they instill in you a sense of wonder?

31 July *Assemble a family tree.* See how far back you can go, how complete you can make it. This activity requires planning and teamwork, talking not only with immediate family but with distant relatives as well.

Make sure you record all births, deaths, marriages, and any other information that portrays the history of your family through its vital statistics. See how many generations you can complete. If you're not sure of certain dates, proceed anyway. Don't get caught up in the details. Your interest in doing this is to see where you've come from, how your family looks on paper, so that all future generations can look back and trace their histories.

When you have done as much as you can, make copies of your family tree and send it to the people who would enjoy seeing their history recorded. Solicit suggestions and information, and incorporate what you find valuable in your next edition. Families can be brought closer through members telling stories about relatives who have passed on. Combined with vital statistics, these tales can comprise an entire family history.

On Giving and Receiving

Society celebrates giving. After all, everyone knows who Mother Teresa is. And when people start to examine themselves, they often talk about how they'd like to be more generous. They think, quite rightly, that a selfless life is a happier life.

But there is another side to the equation that is often overlooked. Receiving is sacred, too. I frequently encounter people who have real difficulty being on the receiving end of another person's offering. It's as if they have identified themselves as givers, have adjusted themselves to the role, and feel uncomfortable in the position of beneficiary of another person's kindness or generosity.

I find these people to be some of the most difficult to please and, often, among the unhappiest people I know. Their obsessive giving allows them to take the moral high ground, to think of themselves as superior to others because of their role as rescuer. They fail to attest to their needs; in fact, they pretend not to have them. They are often life's victims. And at the same time they have lost the ability to delight—in either themselves or others. They seem to want so little for themselves, and take so little pleasure in receiving, that life bypasses them when it hands out its goodies. Everything is a struggle simply because they do not know how to receive.

Being open to receiving—from others, from unexpected sources, from yourself—is a necessary prerequisite for a life filled with happiness. Excessive giving is a dead-end street. When giving is balanced with receiving, when you look for opportunities to receive and give in equal measure, you take pleasure in both. You live your days in reciprocity, with kindness and favors and support flowing freely through your daily life.

August

1 August   *Start a collection.* You can be a traditionalist and gather stamps, coins, or baseball cards, or you can go far beyond the boundaries of convention and collect wild, outlandish things.

The possibilities are endless. You can collect political buttons and/or bumper stickers, coffee mugs, Walt Disney characters, paper clips. Anything will do.

See how many varieties of business cards there are. Matchbooks from restaurants are always a good idea. Things come in different shapes, sizes, and colors. How about collecting shoehorns, felt-tipped pens, frogs? Creativity is working within a certain form to create new content. But sometimes the form is so dramatic that it becomes the content as well.

Wine labels do the job. You don't even have to drink the wine. The value of starting a collection becomes clear later on, when you measure the progress of your creation by tiny incremental changes that at first appear almost imperceptible. But over time, you'll find your collection has changed. It is no longer one or two motley items, but something quite grand.

2 August   *Form a mastermind group.* The purpose of the group is to help you achieve your life goals. Invite at least two people to form the nucleus of the group, and meet on a regular basis. Your meetings do not have to be fre-

quent or formal, but it would be beneficial if they took place at least once every month or so.

The people in your mastermind group could be those whose help to you in the past has been invaluable. They understand you, empathize with you, see your direction as well or even more clearly than you see it yourself. If your dream is to act on Broadway or find a cure for AIDS or learn the restaurant business, the members of your mastermind group could be called upon to consider the steps you are contemplating in pursuit of your objective.

Your goals may change, but your mastermind group remains the same. They are your cheerleaders, your life boosters. Talk to them as frequently as you can. Keep them informed of what's going on in your life. Make sure they're supportive and nonjudgmental, even if they do sometimes suggest courses of action other than those you propose to take.

Offer to serve in their mastermind group. Trade services. Learn from the other members, and be an example for them as well.

3 August   *Think about something you wanted in your life and got.* Was it a pair of roller skates when you were seven? Did you get to drive Dad's car when you took Sally to the junior prom? Were you one of a hundred candidates for your dream job and one day the phone rang and they wanted you?

Remember the feeling you had leading up to the moment you found out you would get your wish, and then the feeling after you found out. What were the sensations like? Did you leap in the air? Cry? Call your best friend and say, "Guess what?" Think about whether you thought you would have your wish granted, about whether you felt you deserved it, how long the feeling of accomplishment lasted, whether you appreciated your good fortune.

Every time you want something great to happen, try to invoke the feeling you had right before something great *did* happen.

4 August   *Read at least two books on the same subject.* If you are pressed for time, read short books. If you'd like to sink your teeth into a topic, seek out the most complete accounts of an event or person or situation you can find, and read them cover to cover.

Let's say you want to find out more about the beginning of Hollywood and the motion picture industry. Start with book one and try to see the author's point of view. While he or she is presenting the facts, he or she is also providing interpretation that gives order to the facts. What is that interpretation? Does it surprise you, or is it pretty much what you had in mind before you read the book?

Now read a second book on the subject. What is this author's point of view? Does it coincide with that of the first book or is it different? How different?

When you're finished, see if you can blend the interpretations you've just read to form your own hypothesis. Talk to other people about your theories. Give them enough information to form an opinion and see what they think.

Immerse yourself in any topic that truly inspires you. Keep reading until you feel you can write something that is your contribution to the subject. You don't actually have to write anything, but the feeling that you *could* is a good one.

5 August   *Write your own obituary.* Think about your life as a whole, about the things you've done that make you most proud, that set you apart from everyone else, that make you unique. Write them down. Don't worry about the order, or whether everyone who knows you would agree that that's really you. Just commit to paper what could be you.

Now think about how you'd like to be remembered. What would you like your grandchildren and great-grandchildren to know about you? Make a list of these qualities. They should indicate the person you are, or maybe the person you are in the process of becoming. Perhaps you are an especially patient supervisor, or have a fine eye for interior design. Make a note.

Compare the two lists. Is what you've done in your life consistent with how you'd like to be remembered? Or is there a gap between expectation and reality?

Now write your obituary. Your perspective is obviously biased, but it is also an intimate one. Keep your obituary updated, and at those times in your life when you feel the old you has shifted, create a new one.

6 August   *Go fishing.* It can be deep-sea fishing, stream fishing, or lake fishing. That's not important. What matters is that you wake up early, while the air still has a slight chill, that you have a friend or two with whom you can spend this day of ultimate leisure, and that your agenda consists of nothing but the pursuit of relaxation.

If you've never gone fishing before, you can get a short book and read up on how it's done. If you don't have gear, you can rent or borrow a rod, reel, and any other equipment you'll need.

The point of fishing is not really to catch fish, although that's ostensibly what you're out there for. The point is to sit and patiently wait for something to happen rather than trying to make it happen. Fishing is the ultimate do-nothing sport. Of course, there is skill involved in bringing the fish in once it has bitten, but that is almost beside the point. Start up a good conversation with your partner, or honor the silence of the early morning hours.

If you do catch a fish, eat it today.

7 August   *Visit a farmers market.* If you don't know of one, ask your local produce store where they buy their fruits and vegetables, call the distributor, and find out where you can buy fresh produce.

Buying fruits and vegetables directly from the grower is a completely different way of shopping. There is no wrapping, no cashiers, no checks, no credit cards, and no delay from field to table. The produce is often picked the day before you buy it.

Buying directly from the farmer also lets you see what's in season, what's locally grown, and what's fresh. It's also cheaper, since there are no middlemen who have to get a percentage of the transaction. Bring your own bags. If you go early in the morning, there is a greater choice; if you go later in the day, you can often get big discounts on produce that will only be thrown away.

If you like good homemade tomato sauce, ask the sellers if they have overripe tomatoes. They'll be only too happy to sell them to you at little cost.

Compared to what we're used to eating, the taste of fresh fruits and vegetables is often profoundly more flavorful. Once you get accustomed to these succulent flavors you may never want to buy produce wrapped in cellophane and shipped from a foreign country again.

8 August   *Kid someone.* This can be a difficult proposition if you're inexperienced, or if you don't know the other person well, but it can work out fine if your intention is

benign—to draw closer to someone or show you've noticed him through humor, and also to show your lighter side.

Humor works on yourself as well. To put yourself on the receiving end of your own joke is an endearing and disarming quality, one that demonstrates to people that you don't take yourself too seriously.

Humor is situational. The context is everything. What's funny to one group or individual can be corny, cutting, or offensive to another, so be careful.

Once, when I was on a cross-country driving trip, I heard a jarring noise every time I hit the brakes. I pulled into a service station and patiently explained the problem to two men who were sitting out front. After hearing my story, they looked at one another, and turned back to me. One of them said, "Brakes are the one thing we haven't learned to do yet." As my face contorted in incredulity, they both had a great big laugh. After a moment I laughed, too.

People are often funnier than they allow themselves to be. And you become funnier when you look for the absurd in normal situations.

9 August   *Make your own homemade ice cream or frozen yogurt.* This is something that will really endear you to your friends, neighbors, colleagues, and any kids who are in your life. It's a perfect activity for a lazy summer afternoon.

You can get an ice-cream maker for very little money, or you can look around in secondhand stores or at garage sales for a used one. The inexpensive ones work very well.

You can find a recipe for making ice cream in any comprehensive cookbook or summer lifestyle magazine. Determine what flavors you want to make—like raspberry chocolate fudge or banana maple walnut—get the ingredients lined up before you start, and then follow the directions.

While you're eating your refreshing concoction, think about how easy the process was, how you don't need to depend on commercial manufacturers to supply you with simple pleasures like this one.

Plan to do this again. Whenever the mood strikes, trot out your machine, cut up some fresh peaches or get some blueberries, and whip up a treat that will make you the talk of your neighborhood or circle of friends.

10 August *Observe a construction site.* Watch something being built. If you look around, you'll probably find a building going up nearby. You only need to spend about twenty minutes looking at the site to get a real sense of what it's like to work as a team on a project, with everyone doing a different job on different areas of the structure. And somehow, it all comes together in the end.

Don't get too close. It's not only dangerous, but you'll lose your perspective on the whole. The best way to see how a site works is to watch from afar, to see the interplay of people and machinery that combines to create something out of nothing, that can take the vision of a few individuals, translate it into a concrete plan that can be read by many more, and then be constructed by even greater numbers.

Visit the site from time to time to see how much progress is being made. Does it feel like watching a baby grow? Can you see the development from a hole in the ground, to a foundation, to the lower floors, to the upper floors, to the outer shell, then the roof and finish work?

If you're really interested, go to the trailer on site and talk to whoever's in charge. Ask questions. Find out if you can put on a hard hat and take a little tour of the area. Chances are he or she will be glad to show you around for a few minutes.

11 August   *Attend a rehearsal.* It could be a ballet, opera, symphony, play, or the practice session of a combo that plays down the street at a neighborhood bar or club. What you're trying to do is see how a performance comes together, what process takes place to make it appear as if the actual performance were effortless.

When you sit in the theater or hall watching the players rehearse, see if there is clearly a leader. Does one person take charge? Does everyone else acknowledge this person, or are there some tensions that surface from time to time? Does the rehearsal have a structure? Is one specific part being drilled, or is it a matter of practicing the entire performance together to get a sense of what this piece should feel like?

Can you see the performance come together? Can you see progress? Or do you sit there in amazement, wondering how this group is ever going to perform at anything close to professional level? If you close your eyes, can you see or hear the actual performance? Don't overlook the enjoyment of the music or the acting you're actually experiencing.

If you can, go backstage and talk to some of the performers. If you are curious after attending the rehearsal, go to the real thing. Hear the polished performance and compare it to what you heard before.

If it's inconvenient for you to witness a live rehearsal, see the movie *Meeting Venus*.

12 August *Spend time in a bookstore.* There are a variety of choices you can make, depending on your mood. The big chain bookstores have the latest and most popular books; there are used and secondhand bookstores for those who want something rarer; academic bookstores cater to people who are interested in intellectual pursuits; and, often, your city or town will have specialty bookstores— poetry, mystery, metaphysics, science fiction, or children's books.

As soon as you cross the threshold of the store, you enter into a new world, one in which information, knowledge, even wisdom, reside. Try to feel the atmosphere of the store. Can you easily pick up a book and flip through it without feeling pressured to buy? Are the shelves organized so that books are easy to find? Are the employees helpful? Do they know books and are they willing to look up titles to help you locate something?

If you are browsing in a bookstore that sells popular books, see what is on the minds of writers—and readers— today. What are the themes or general interests of writers? Is there something that unites them, or are the books in the stores moving in many directions? Look at the design of the covers. Do some draw you in, while others discourage you from picking them up? What about titles? Do they reveal the meaning of the books and make you want to read them, or do they seem inappropriate and lackluster?

Wander around. Saunter up and down the aisles. Look at a picture of the author on a book jacket and see if you're attracted to this person, if you'd like to have a conversation with him or her. If you would, you might also like to read the book he or she has written.

If a book keeps jumping out at you, or you find yourself returning to it, chances are there's something in its pages that is speaking to you and from which you might benefit.

13 August   *Attend a service of a different faith.* If you are Roman Catholic, attend a Jewish or evangelical Baptist service. Or, if you are a Jew, visit the congre-

gation of a Protestant denomination, or, better yet, go to an Islamic temple and be a part of Moslem prayer.

Try going to a Zen temple or monastery, a service of the Baha'i faith, or a Korean Presbyterian church. Just tell the members of the congregation that you practice another faith and would like to sit and observe their service. They'll likely welcome you.

While you're there, try to see the similarities between your faith and the one you're visiting, but also be aware of the differences. In the end, is the spirit of the service and the people the same as your own faith's? Reflect upon the fact that people everywhere are committing atrocities in the name of their particular faith, and have done so for thousands of years. See if you can come up with one way you can help bridge the gap between faiths, to help people understand that they are more alike than they are different.

Thank the minister, priest, rabbi, or whoever was in charge of the service, and invite him or her to your house of worship as your personal guest.

14 August   *Visit a factory.* See how something is made. It can be a brewery, a chocolate factory, a computer assembly plant, or a place where durable goods are manufactured. Take the time to watch the process, to learn how something starts out in one form and becomes another.

Most factories will provide a guided tour if you call ahead. And some have regularly scheduled tours. The guides are usually very informative and will answer questions with skill.

At the end of the tour there may even be a free sample of what you've just seen manufactured, assembled, or transformed. The staff will do its best to make you feel at home, and to tell you how you can learn more about the manufacturing of the product.

Seeing how something is made often demystifies the process. You can understand how an item or gadget logically fits together. You'll also see the myriad steps that you never dreamed were essential to its completion.

So, too, with life. There are innumerable processes that are required to live in happiness and fulfillment, and it helps to know how they fit together.

15 August   *Release your frustration physically.* Every life, no matter how tranquil, uneventful, or predictable, has frustration. In fact, the calmer the life, the more the little things can produce irritation.

Sometimes the symptoms are oblique—like boredom, general anxiety, and brusqueness. Or they can be physical, taking the form of headaches, and back, shoulder, or neck pain.

You have a number of options. You can organize a game of rough touch football. You can pound a pillow, put on goggles and break something—like a brick—to bits with a sledgehammer, or wrestle with a buddy. If you feel you want to release this frustration on a regular basis, get one of those blow-up plastic dummies that always returns to standing when you strike it, or buy a pair of boxing gloves and a punching bag and have at it. You'll feel great. And it doesn't take long. You won't have to do it for more than several minutes to begin to release the frustration that's built up.

16 August   *Make a tape for a friend or relative.* It can be video or audio, but if you choose the video route you'll have to come up with some interesting visuals to make the tape compelling for the viewer.

If you just want to communicate with someone, sit down with a fresh tape in a tape recorder and collect your thoughts for a moment. A half hour's worth of taping should suffice. Test the level of the recording, and start talking into the machine as if the person to whom you were speaking was right there with you.

Start by explaining what you've been doing, and gradually move into how you feel about it. You can talk about work or family life, your views on the state of the world, or the changes you've made since you last corresponded.

Every time you feel at a loss for words, or are confused about what you want to say, simply press "pause." You can make your tape over several days or do it in one sitting. Whatever you decide, make sure you complete the project. Don't let it go. The more you open up, the easier you'll find it to talk. Relate the past, talk about the present, share your dreams about the future.

You can send the tape in the box in which it came. Just address it, stamp it, and mail it. Sending a tape is a wonderful way to communicate over a long distance. A videocassette of your growing children is a most cherished gift for grandparents across the country.

Then, if you are so inclined, invite the person to whom you are reaching out to respond.

17 August   *Go on a bicycle ride.* If you don't have a bicycle, you can rent or borrow one. If you haven't been on a bicycle in years, don't worry. As they say, once you learn . . . it will come back to you quickly.

You can go on a long trip, or just around the neighborhood. You can go alone, or with a friend, your spouse, or your kids. It's a good idea to wear a helmet. (You can rent or borrow these, too.)

A wonderful time to go is early in the morning or during the early evening, when the heat is not at its peak. Ride on the right side of the road, observe all traffic signals, and ride single file on busy streets.

If you rode a lot as a child, see if you can recapture the feeling of freedom you had when you were eleven years old and you jumped on your bicycle. Feel the wind rushing through your hair as you go downhill at a pretty good speed, and see how quickly you can get places without the hassle of parking.

Pack a snack and ride to a nearby park. Or plan to be out the whole day and really make your trip a workout. Or run your daily errands on your bicycle.

When you return, as you park your bike realize that freedom is available to you at any time. You can just hop on and take off for as long—or short—as you want.

18 August *Get together with people you used to work with.* Have lunch, or go out for a drink or bite to eat after work. Invite a few people, and when you are together see if you easily get back into the dialogue, the concerns, the rhythm of what it was like to work with these people.

How do you feel about seeing them? Do you miss them? Are they more concerned about telling you what's going on with them than they are about finding out what's going on with you? Is the conversation positive or negative? Have things changed since you worked at the company or have they pretty much stayed the same?

Could you ever go back? Would you want to go back, or have you progressed beyond that job, that place, these people? Do you like the person you've become since you left? Can you measure your progress? Does it make sense to you that you ever worked in that environment, or does it all have a feeling that it was someone else's life?

19 August *Start a garden.* If you have a back-yard, that's the perfect place to plant it. If you don't know where to begin, ask someone who knows gardening to help you. Gardeners are usually delighted to share their knowledge. Or read a beautiful book on gardening that inspires you to begin.

Flowers and vegetables are a wonderful way to start. You can get bulbs and seeds, or buy potted flowers and vegetables that have already been started and plant them. Make sure you get information on what works best in your climate and soil so that you give your garden the greatest chance of succeeding.

If you don't have a backyard, find out about a community garden in which you can take part. This is a great opportunity to learn more about gardening or share your enthusiasm and expertise with others. Seniors and teenagers mix with middle-aged mothers and fathers to plant all kinds of interesting, delicious things.

If your community doesn't have a garden, contact your local parks and recreation department and start lobbying to establish one.

20 August *If you have a computer, clean out your files.* Go through your entire set of documents and

delete what you don't need; if you use a hard-disk drive, take files off the hard disk and put them on floppies.

As you go through each file, try to remember the moment you created it, what it meant to you, how meaningful it was to you. But don't hold on to something that you know you're never going to use again. Or, if you are attached to it, make a hard copy of a document and then delete it.

If your files are reasonably up to date and you don't need to do any housekeeping, learn a new program. Add something to your repertoire. See if you can raise your level of expertise a notch.

If you've never used a computer, find out how one works. Sit down at a keyboard with someone who knows her way around and practice some simple applications.

Or, if you're intimidated by computers, ask the young son or daughter of a friend to teach you a computer game or show you a graphic arts program that is fun and exciting. Sometimes the way into the world of computers is easier than you think.

21 August *Take a train ride.* If trains are a part of your regular commute, and the opportunity is convenient, take an overnight train ride. If this is not, get on a train, find a seat by the window, and watch the countryside move by without having to concentrate on driving, or on anything for that matter.

Feel the excitement as you wait for the train in the station. Notice the looks of anticipation on the faces of the passengers. Check the arrivals and departures board to see what track your train is leaving from.

Get on the train early. Find a comfortable spot, pull out a magazine to flip through while you're waiting to depart, and listen to the sounds that the train makes even before it begins to move.

Notice the people on the train. Are they anxious or relaxed, talkative or quiet? How about you? Are you thinking about your trip, your destination, or the everyday life you are temporarily leaving behind?

Once the train is in motion, wander through the various cars. Spend time in the dining car, the club car, and, if you've booked a cabin, luxuriate in it.

Get off at a few of the train's stops, even for a minute, just to see what a different location feels like. When you return to the train, see if you can identify the new passengers, and notice whether the train takes on a different energy each time it stops.

22 August *Deepen your intuition.* Find out more about it. What is intuition? Where does it come from? Is it the same as instinct? Gut feeling? Why is it said that women have better intuition than men? Do you find that to be true?

Everyone has a capacity for heightened intuition, but very few of us use it. There are some life situations, however, that call for intuitive rather than intellectual knowledge, so it helps to know how to avail yourself of both.

The first step in developing your intuitive sense is to think of something that puzzles you, ask for guidance, and then sit quietly. This may be more difficult than you think, but if you can be still for a few moments your conscious mind will move to the background, allowing your intuitive mind to confront the problem. Don't expect instant results. Intuition requires practice.

Do this every day for a week and you will have begun to develop the habit of checking with your intuitive mind to look for answers to your life's problems. Pick up one of the many books on the subject, like Nancy Rosanoff's *Intuition Workout.* Familiarize yourself with other techniques that will make intuition a more integral part of your life. In time, this form of knowledge will blend with the others you already use.

23 August   *Get your shoes shined.* You have two choices: You can do the job yourself; or you can go to a shoemaker, a street corner, the airport, or a train terminal and get them shined by a professional for a couple of dollars per pair, depending on what part of the country you live in.

If you do it yourself you can use liquid polish and apply it directly to your shoes, or use solid polish and a shoe brush and chamois. This takes some time, but it's worth it. You can look down and admire the spectacular job you've done. Your shoes will look like you just bought them.

If you go to a professional, there are other pleasures. You can sit high in the chair and carry on a conversation with the person shining your shoes. Or you can read a newspaper or magazine, feeling your feet getting a slight workout as your shoes are being whipped into shape. You will feel wealthy, accomplished, important.

Having your shoes shined and polished will get you noticed. It is said that in Italy people give others the once-over from the ground up. Remember that. The shine on your shoes makes a real statement. It might be a good idea to invest in new soles and heels, too.

It is also said that some single people choose their partners by the shoes they wear and the condition in which they find them. Don't lose out. Remember: feet first.

24 August   *Spend a whole day watching people, as if you were a cub reporter whose assignment was to learn as much as you could about people just from watching them.* From the time you get up in the morning, watch your family, and continue watching the people with whom you come into contact for the rest of the day.

Notice their mannerisms, the way they speak, the tone of their voices, the way they dress, carry themselves, how well they make eye contact. Are people mostly happy or unhappy? Do they seem to be at ease with themselves, or do you notice a general level of discomfort in those with whom you come into contact?

Observe these people without judgment. Don't say to yourself that the color of the salesperson's tie is all wrong, or that you like the smell of the perfume of your co-worker in the next cubicle. Just watch, observe, listen, feel, taste, and smell as if you had no critical faculty, no way of evaluating what you experience.

At the end of the day, how do you feel? Are you energized? Allow yourself the luxury of one categorization, one broad generalization you felt from your day's worth of observation. What is it?

25 August *Make plans to attend an amusement park, circus, or state fair.* You might want to take your kids, your neighbor's kids, or your niece and nephew with you.

Amusement parks are places for people, rides, games, indulging in junk food, and laughter. You can visit exhibitions, try to win a stuffed animal or other prizes in contests of skill or luck, or buy a handcrafted jewelry box.

You can stay all day or for just an hour. Enjoy the carnival music. Perhaps there will be a magic show or puppets. The entire enterprise is organized to take you far, far away from your normal routine. Submit to it.

26 August *Conduct a science experiment.* Remember the time in the eighth grade when your science teacher put together two liquids and smoke came out of the test tube, or when your next-door neighbor mixed two compounds and created a sparkler. Try to re-create the feeling of that time by conducting a small experiment.

One easy one is to fill up a glass of water and place a three-by-five card on the rim. Now turn over the glass and see what happens. Another neat idea is for two people to take off their shoes and slide around a carpeted room. After a few minutes you can touch each other and demonstrate the principle of static electricity.

Are you ready for an optical illusion? Hold the middle of a pencil or pen loosely between your thumb and forefinger. Now lazily move your arm as if you were using a salt shaker. What happens to the pencil? Does it look like it's made out of rubber? You can really impress kids with this demonstration of trompe l'oeil.

See if you can come up with another way to confirm that things aren't always what they appear to be. Unseen forces exist, and realizing that they do is the first step in exploring them further. Think about the connection between mind and matter. What is more real, an idea or a material representation of it?

27 August   *Cuddle with someone.* It could be your lover, but it could also be your brother or sister, child, niece, nephew, or your dog. Cuddling can be very therapeutic.

First, pick a comfortable spot, preferably one in which the temperature is just right. If you can be outdoors, on a lounge chair perhaps, the elements can add immeasurably to your satisfaction.

Just lie there in each other's arms. This is not meant to arouse, only to soothe. Quiet talk about things that interest both of you will enhance the moment. But silence is also fitting.

28 August   *Get your résumé together.* If you don't have a current one, start assembling the information you need to make a representative document of your work history and aspirations. Make sure it includes your present situation and all the skills and experiences that would interest a prospective employer.

If you don't know how to start, there are dozens of books that can show you how. Having a résumé says you are ready to take full advantage of any opportunity that crosses your path. It lets you—and anyone who is interested in you—know that you are capable of marketing yourself in the workplace so as to secure a position that is commensurate with your abilities and earning power.

Your résumé doesn't have to be pretty as long as it is neatly typed, easy to read, specific, and never longer than two pages. Remember, your résumé is a summary of your work history, not the third chapter of the Book of Genesis. Anyone who reads it should know immediately what you are capable of doing and whether you potentially fit a current or future opening.

Your résumé should accomplish only two goals: to help the person reading it decide whether he or she wants to meet you, and to help you organize and acknowledge all your skills and accomplishments. When you send out your résumé, make sure a cover letter accompanies it.

29 August   *Look for signs of fall.* Despite boiling temperatures and saunalike humidity, see if you can detect the early signals that a new season is in the offing.

Is the air in the morning a little chillier than it was a month ago, even though the afternoons are just as hot? Does a slight breeze whip up in the afternoon, with the promise of a much cooler one a month from now? How about the clouds? What do they look like? Do they still hold their fluffy summer pattern, or is the sky showing the first signs of winter storms?

Look closely at the light. Does the angle of the sun as it reflects off the ground or a window or a clump of trees remind you of another season?

Do leaves rustle on the branches of trees, even though they haven't yet turned or fallen? Does the air have a different quality from that which it had in July? Keep watching, and within days you'll see unmistakable signs that another season is ushering itself in.

30 August   *Do a puzzle.* There are a variety of word puzzles in most newspapers and even if you are not in the habit of looking at them, try one or two and see how far you get.

Or do a jigsaw puzzle. You can commit to a long-term project and buy a thousand-piece puzzle of Big Ben, or start out small with a hundred- or two-hundred-fifty-piece puzzle of animals or a snow scene. First, turn over all the pieces onto the picture side and get the outside edges of the puzzle together. Then work on one part of the puzzle until you've completed it. Invite someone over to help you.

Puzzles can provide valuable insight into life. It's going to take you some time to complete the puzzle, and you'll get there faster the more you work on it, although there are times when your frustration level may get too high and you'll have to take a break.

The puzzle will teach you creativity, the awareness that you may have to try many different combinations before finding the pieces that fit. It's just like life: it requires practice, patience, concentration, and commitment—and surrender.

31 August   *Ask for a raise at work.* Test the waters. See where your boss stands on the subject of your performance by asking for more money.

One of the objectives of this activity is to ask for what you want. Don't assume that the universe is going to provide it for you because you are needy and deserving and you have more medical bills than you can handle. You've got to ask for what you want.

Make sure you know why you deserve this raise. If you can base your request on what you've produced for the company you automatically strengthen your case.

Keep in mind that employers do not want to lose good employees and will usually do whatever it takes, including awarding raises, to keep them. The best way to get a raise is to ask for a specific amount, say 15 percent. That way, even if your boss does not want to agree to the full request, he or she may feel compelled to give you something.

If you're the boss, be prepared to handle your employees' requests by thinking about their performances. Keep in mind that the more you provide, the more you'll get in return.

Pain Is Not the Enemy

One of the biggest mistakes people make when they are trying to incorporate more happiness into their lives is avoidance of pain. They plan and execute intricate, involved strategies to remove themselves from difficult life situations that they think are opposite of what they're trying to achieve. Nothing could be farther from the truth.

Trying to live your life avoiding pain is itself one of the most painful paths you can take. It is bound to fail as a life strategy, since pain and suffering and hardship, either physical or emotional, are an inevitable part of the human landscape. But even if never-ending pain avoidance was possible, it would be a counterproductive way of living.

For the reality is that you never *really* avoid pain, you never *really* don't feel it, and you never *really* insulate yourself from the repercussions of how your being is reacting to a painful situation. You may bury it in some remote part of yourself that appears to be far from the surface, but it never is. Pain grows if it is not acknowledged. It can manifest itself in backaches, heart disease, cancer, or merely in an inability to experience any feelings at all, the highs *or* the lows.

Happiness is surely not the absence of pain. It is not a life cut off from the reality of disappointment, discomfort, disease, and injustice. In order to be as joyful as you are capable of being, acknowledge when you are feeling less than good, at least to yourself, and try to see the feeling not as an enemy, but an ally. You'll be surprised at how much less painful the feeling eventually becomes. Working *through* the pain, not around it, to the pleasure at the other end, is a healthier course of action.

September

1 September   *Doodle.* The best time to doodle is while you're talking on the telephone, so that the other person isn't aware that you're not giving him or her your complete attention, but business meetings are also a good time.

Doodling serves a variety of functions. Most importantly, it gets you in touch with your unconscious, the place where your secret desires are stored. When you let your mind wander, when you allow your hand to move in any direction it chooses, you are expressing your true nature. Pay attention to that. It could be important.

Doodling also allows you to pass time when you are not fully engaged. You can become engaged in your doodling instead. It is often a great way of combating boredom or frustration, and doodling the same pattern, like circles with curlicues, can have a mesmerizing effect.

Do your doodles have any transcendental meaning to you? Do they remind you of someone or something? Do they evoke a mood or feeling? Keep your favorites and look back at them occasionally. Have your doodles changed over the years?

2 September   *Let loose.* Pull out all the stops today and do things you never thought you'd have the audacity to do. If a key to healthy living is in the saying "Everything in moderation—including moderation," make this the day

you moderate your moderation. Go to extremes. Eat nothing but potato chips at every meal. Have chocolate cake at midnight. Take a three-hour lunch break at work, or better still, take a ride in the country.

Your mission today is to throw caution out the window. Everything that tells you what you should or should not do is to be ignored. The only thing that matters is that you let yourself follow your unbridled yearnings. Do you like to spend time on the telephone? Have marathon phone conversations with your friends. Do you feel good when you are generous to people? Make today the day you go out and buy a present for everyone you love. Pretend it's Christmas. Don't wait for the "right" time. The right time is now.

Do you love to dance? Go out and don't come back until you drop. Do you make model airplanes? Immerse yourself in your passions. Keep going. Make yourself an instrument through which the love of these passions expresses itself.

By the end of the day, it's important to feel there isn't a single thing you still need to do. Your desire to indulge should be satisfied.

3 September   *Organize a potluck dinner.* The more people you invite, the greater the variety of dishes and the bigger the feast. But small gatherings can also be creative and fun.

You can make it a real potluck and not give the people you've invited any instructions as to what to bring. It will be a great surprise, and if you end up having six salads and no main course, well, that's just the luck of the pot. Or you can meticulously plan the menu so that the dishes are perfectly balanced. It's up to you.

During dinner you and your guests will be treated to the most imaginative concoctions of everyone assembled. Each loving creation will contribute to the excitement of the event.

To make sure you don't get stuck doing all the cleaning up, include some kind of chore as part of the dinner. With a large party this should not be a problem. Tell people to bring small quantities of food. With so many choices, people usually want to sample everything, and small quantities will reduce the temptation to load up on any one dish.

You can spice up the event even more by having everyone share a funny food story from his or her past.

4 September *Play the role of devil's advocate.*
For one day, take the position opposite of any you hear expounded, regardless of the position you normally hold. You can inform the person with whom you are discussing that you're taking the other side for the sport of it, or you can pretend that you actually believe what you're saying.

See what it feels like to take the other side, to argue with equal fervor against something you might deeply hold to be true. What do your usual arguments sound like when you hear them expressed by someone else? Are you more comfortable holding the opposite view than you thought you would be? Or do you find it just as wrong, just as obnoxious, as you did when you were motivated to express your true feelings?

Debating from the other side will help clarify your own position. Any idea, any thought, that has become stale will immediately jump out at you when you hear it uttered by someone else. It's a good idea to know the other side of a question. When you allow the plausibility of the opposing argument, when you cultivate a more detached view without sacrificing your passion, your positions become much sharper, more focused and compassionate than they were before.

5 September   *Pretend it's a new year.* When you were a school kid September meant the beginning of the term. No matter how well or poorly you did in the past, you had the opportunity to start out fresh, to excel, to prove to everyone, including yourself, that you were capable of impressing your teachers and classmates with your performance.

Start something new. Wipe the slate of your life clean; get a brand new notebook, fill it with unused white sheets of paper, and set lofty goals for yourself. Don't wait for January. Now is as good a time as any to go for the highest marks in life.

Make time work for you, not against you. Tell yourself constantly that you have enough time to do whatever it is you have a hankering for. Start doing what you want to do, even if it's the middle of the week. Resolve that your life is your creation and that you can make or do or be anything you want to make or do or be.

6 September   *Go to a trade show or convention.* It doesn't have to be in your profession, although it might be. You can do this in either of two ways. If you have the means to travel, find out where a show featuring one of your interests is being held and go there. If you love computers, you may end up flying to Atlanta or Las Vegas to spend three days immersed in motherboards and software. If your interest is women's apparel, Dallas or New York or Chicago might be your ticket.

If you would like to remain close to home, ask your local chamber of commerce for a listing of the trade shows being held in your area. The list usually covers a year's schedule of shows, and you might be surprised to find out that your interest in cars can be satisfied very close by.

At the show, walk down the aisles and get a feel for the energy, the excitement, of all the different goods and services that are being offered in this industry alone. A trade show can be overwhelming, but if you move through once and get an idea of what's there, you can concentrate later on the displays that excite you.

People who work the booths will be happy to give you free samples, a demonstration of their product, and any kind of information you seek. That's their job. Don't spend any time with people who aren't friendly. A trade show is one place you don't have to tolerate rudeness.

By attending, you'll undoubtedly come away with a greater awareness of the cutting-edge trends and developments in the business that interests you. And you'll refresh that interest by being among people who share your enthusiasm.

7 September   *Buy a new tool.* Think of a project you've been meaning to start. It can be big or little, in the house, garden, or yard, on your car or at work. Whatever you've been contemplating, have a new tool in mind and get it—your job will be easier and you'll be motivated to get going.

The tool can be as small as a screwdriver or as big as a bulldozer. Do you want to plant new flowers or prune your trees? Get a new spade, hoe, or set of pruning shears. Have you been thinking about building a bookcase for your child's room? Look at the power saws, sanders, or even something as small as a T square.

When you shop for your new tool, ask the person who works in the store to explain the different features of your alternatives. Do you need an open-ended whisk, a closed-ended whisk, or a food processor? Think about your budget, the project you want to complete, and any other projects you may want to do in the future. Buy the tool that suits your needs. It may not be something you use every time you cook, build, or garden, but it should be an important addition to your array of tools. It should in some way enhance your ability to carry out more tasks and to make what you like to do easier, more efficient, and more fun.

8 September   *Organize a group effort and manage the project.* Have you been thinking for years of replacing the fence around your front yard? You can do it now, with much less effort than you might think, if you can get a team together.

Write down your objective on paper. State the time by which you want to have the project completed. Write down each task and estimate how long you think it will take to do.

Now make a list of the people whom you could ask to help you. Call them and ask if they're interested in helping you replace your fence. Read them the list of things that have to be done, and ask if any appeals to them.

Press for a commitment. If you get one, inquire if they know someone who also might be interested. Pick a time and get everyone together. Be the foreman. Direct the team. Praise the work as much as you can. People perform better with encouragement. It's easier to draw bees with honey than it is with vinegar.

If fence-building seems inconsequential, think about building a teen center, or organizing a lobbying effort to make your neighborhood safer.

9 September   *Pray for something you want to have happen.* Whether you beseech God, Buddha, the Universe, or some other deity, apply yourself to the task of asking for divine help.

Praying at night is the most traditional time for prayer, but you can pray at any time of the day. Walk around and silently repeat your prayer, or visit a house of worship and pray in the bosom of a religious institution. The particular setting is not significant. What matters is that you apply your will for as long as it takes to have your prayers answered. To change circumstances that seem intractable, you will have to apply yourself for a long time. Start now.

Napoleon Hill, the author of *Think and Grow Rich,* had a son who was born without ears. The doctors told him that this boy would never hear. After four years of concentrated prayer, it was clear that the boy could hear. By the time he entered college, he had 65 percent of normal hearing—without ears—and then a device was designed for him, giving him 100 percent hearing.

Prayer is a demonstration of faith, and faith can move mountains.

10 September   *Don't answer your phone.* Let it ring. Even if you are home, pretend you're not there. If you have an answering machine, let it pick up your calls, or unplug the phone if you find it impossible to be home and not answer the phone.

Before the telephone was invented, people were not available for instant communication. Messages were received by post or messenger. Now, everyone is tied to the phone. It's an instrument of communication, but it's also an instrument of intrusion.

You *can* do something to control the flow of information into your life. You can regulate how much you want to interact with people. Not answering your phone is a demonstration of your ability to set limits in your environment.

Ignoring your ringing phone breaks the normal rhythm of your life. It pulls you out of the mode of being instantly available to everyone who seeks you out. It gives you a glimpse of what life was like before electronic communications took over, when days were more drawn out, and people stayed with activities for more than a few minutes at a time.

11 September   *Imagine you had all the money you wanted.* Perhaps you just won the lottery, or inherited a fortune from a rich aunt you never knew existed, or woke up one morning with an idea that was developed into a multimillion-dollar project. What would you do with your life? What would you do with the money?

How would you spend your time—or your money, for that matter? Do you feel confident that you could intelligently deal with that vast sum, or do you fear you'd go through it so fast that it would be almost as if you never had it?

Do you have a wish list of things you'd buy, places you'd visit, organizations to which you'd lend your financial support, individuals to whom you might give a start in life? If not, make your list now. Act as if the money has just been given to you and it's time to figure out what to do with it.

When you act as if something you want to happen has already happened, you help bring it about. If you start helping people, even without enormous sums of money, in ways that you can afford, you create conditions in your life for more money to come in. Live your life as if the money were already there. Don't be seduced by the illusion of "reality." Reality is whatever you think it is.

12 September   *Send a postcard to yourself.*

Act as if you are on vacation and are writing to someone you know very well back home. The postcard can be from a faraway place, one that you picked up from a trip you took some time ago, or it could be from the town in which you live.

Sit down and write to yourself. Let yourself know how well you're doing, what kind of days you've been having, where you've been, with whom you've been spending time, where your itinerary will take you next. Be as creative as you like. Indulge your fantasies and make up stories, or describe in detail what your day has consisted of.

When you receive the card, see if you still feel like the sender, the same way you did when you wrote it, or if you want to change into the recipient who has stayed back and now awaits word from long-distance. Read the card as if you had never seen it before, as if you've been waiting anxiously to hear from yourself.

Imagine being in the place where the card originated, perhaps with azure water and white sandy beaches all around, having a great time, eager to get back and tell everyone how your trip went.

13 September   *Read the Bible as literature.* See it as a book, not as the word of God, and read it as a story of a particular people in a particular time and place.

Recognize that this is the most important work of western civilization. Pretend you are a time traveler and have come across this book. Read a chapter from the Old Testament and one from the New Testament, and see if the stories make sense as a narrative whole, not as the basis for a religion.

What feelings are evoked? How does the story sound to you? Is it believable? Preposterous? Can you spot divine presence behind the words? Make sure the language of your version is one that you can readily understand. Does the portion you are reading have modern themes, or is it clearly about different people in different times? Why do you think this book became so popular, especially during the last five hundred years? Was it the invention of the printing press? The translation of the book into languages other than Latin?

Make the book come alive, so it doesn't simply remain a relic that is trotted out on Saturdays, Sundays, or holidays and then put back on the shelf.

14 September *Stay home all day.* Don't leave the house. Plan activities that will allow you to putter around, make little repairs, do household chores, or just relax in your living space.

You can read, write, watch television, listen to music, take a long, hot bath, cook, clean, talk to friends, relatives, or acquaintances (either in person or over the telephone), pay bills, catch up on paperwork, or daydream.

Make sure you have enough to eat, or order food from a place that will deliver to your home. This idea works best if the weather is rainy, but even a beautiful day will allow you to feel comfortable, secure, in possession of your life. It will feel as if time has slowed down, and that you can move from one thing to the next without feeling rushed.

If you spend the whole day at home, you'll also know your house or apartment better than you did yesterday, regardless of how long you have lived in it. Let it be your castle, protective and all encompassing.

15 September   *Eat popcorn for dinner.*
Make as much as you want, share it with some friends or relatives, and make a meal out of it. If popcorn isn't your favorite, then eat grapes or something else easy to prepare.

See if you can eat enough of a single food to satisfy you, and allow yourself the thought that you can do whatever you want, that there are no conventions or customs to which you must strictly adhere.

See how much more time you have without having to prepare and clean up dinner. What can you do instead with this time? Can you share a massage or a good conversation? Put aside the time you normally devote to cooking for some other kind of treat, besides food.

16 September   *Ask for directions.* This is especially important if you're a man, for by doing so you will dispel the machismo of which so many women complain. "They will not ask for directions" is something that women say about men when they want to express dissatisfaction with the entire gender.

Asking for directions proves that you are not alone, that local inhabitants are a great resource, and that people are usually willing to help. (Some people will repeat directions, word for word, just to make sure you understand them.)

Asking for directions doesn't always work. Some friends and I were driving one evening and got very lost in the heart of Queens, New York. We spotted an older man walking his dog, and asked for directions. He tried several times to explain where to go—unsuccessfully—threw up his hands in desperation, and finally told us to ditch the car and take a taxi.

But asking for directions often is the intelligent alternative to wandering around on your own. It simply minimizes wasted time. It also connects you with others, allows you to practice asking for what you want, and gets you where you want to go faster.

17 September   *Look through your personal archives.* You may keep them in cardboard boxes, photo albums, or scrapbooks, in the garage, attic, or basement. You may have them stored in shoe boxes, cigar boxes, or neatly filed in folders, their contents meticulously typed on color-coded tabs. However your archives are organized—or disorganized—sit down and look through them carefully and lovingly.

Be fully aware of what each piece means to you, why you chose to save it, the kind of feeling it evokes in you. If you have children who are old enough to appreciate the past, this might be a good way to introduce them to yours.

If you find that a certain piece no longer has any meaning for you, discard it. Or move it to another box, one that occupies the second rung in your archival life.

When you look through your archives, you can linger for as long as you want on any piece or item. A letter from a special friend can be read and digested with as much pleasure as a great meal or a fine wine. If you allow the memories to materialize, you will be literally inundated with the feelings and impressions of the past.

You certainly don't have to go through everything you've saved. Sometimes you just want to get in touch with a particular time and can go directly to what reminds you of that. On other occasions you may want to stop at a point that seems to correspond to where you are right now.

18 September   *Visit a university or college campus.* Since this is probably the beginning of the semester, you'll feel the excitement of the first few days of school, when every student displays the nervous anticipation of the impending term.

Get a feel for the campus. Is it large, noisy, urban, bustling, or does it have a quiet, compelling, contained nature? Is the school known for its parties, or its scholarship? Does it draw from an international pool of students, or is it state run and state focused?

Walk around the heart of the campus, going from building to building. Visit a dormitory. Sit on a lawn and try to fathom what the students you see are thinking about. Ask a few what they intend to study, what they plan to pursue when they graduate.

Visit the school library. (You may have to get special permission to do this.) See if you can remember when you were a student, what it felt like, what your dreams were. Did you turn out to be the person you thought you would be?

Sit in on a class of your choice. Have you always been fascinated with physics, or has English literature or life drawing been your unfulfilled passion? Think about the effort that goes into dissemination of knowledge at the higher levels, the thinking, reading, writing, and evaluation. How can learning something new enrich your life? What are the benefits that go beyond the information itself?

19 September   *Start a tradition.* Do something on the same day, in the same way, with the same people, in the same sequence, and take note of the ways in which you are keeping the tradition alive.

Have the same dish in the same restaurant every year on your wedding anniversary. Take your kids to the same park every Saturday morning and play Frisbee or soccer. Starting a tradition anchors you to the present, provides positive continuity, and puts you in touch with the natural order of things. Just as trees bear blossoms and then leaves at the same time every year, implement weekly, monthly, or yearly traditions.

Make Friday the night you eat Chinese food or rent movies, or Sunday the day you call your parents. A balanced mixture of tradition and spontaneity can combine to create a happy, healthy life. It's reassuring to have things to count on in a world of constant change.

20 September *Test-drive your fantasy car.* This is an opportunity to get what you want, if only for a short time, to see if it's really you.

If you want to make an even bigger statement than the test drive, rent the vehicle for a day, and pretend that it's really your car. How does it feel to cruise around in that red convertible Alfa Romeo, or that sleek Jaguar you've been thinking about since you were fourteen years old?

Maybe your dream vehicle is a four-wheel-drive Jeep, or a pickup truck. Rent it. Be with it. Drive it around and see how you feel about it at the end of one day. In just twenty-four hours you'll know if your fantasy was justified, or if reality just didn't measure up to your image of it.

Even if your everyday routine consists of two kids and a station wagon, you can be a completely different person for a spell if you decide to bop around town in a '65 cherry Mustang. Make sure your car comes equipped with a great stereo.

21 September *Make an overseas phone call.* If you know someone in a foreign country—a friend, a distant cousin, a close relative who is vacationing—call her up

and talk to her. Even if you don't know anyone, pick a country and call a hotel, or the tourist bureau for information.

Find out when it's cheapest to call, and make sure you allow for time-zone differences. Call your long-distance carrier and ask for the country code for, let's say, India. There is usually also a city code. You can dial direct most of the time.

Overseas hotels usually have toll-free 800 numbers. Call them up, ask about the weather or what's going on there, and tell them where you are and what's going on where you live.

When you dial the fifteen or so digits, you'll feel the excitement of connecting with people halfway around the world. You'll hear the signal go through, that unmistakable sound of connection about to be made, and then the unfamiliar ring.

If your call is answered by someone who doesn't speak English, and no one around does, try another number or country.

22 September   *Imagine your death.* Think seriously about how you would like to pass on, under what circumstances. What conditions feel right to you? How long do you want to live? All these considerations are more in your control than you've been taught to think.

Do you want to expire quietly and unexpectedly— robust, healthy, and vibrant up to the very end? Or do you want your last days to be occupied with the people you love most tearfully saying good-bye as you slowly slip from this realm into another?

Imagining your own death makes the whole process that much less frightening. Everything is less fearsome when it is faced rather than denied. If you want to live to be eighty-five years old, you have a high probability of doing just that. If you imagine yourself living long in this lifetime, you will make decisions that support that desire.

Twenty-five hundred years ago Socrates said that it was foolish to fear something that you really didn't know anything about. Overwhelming fear of death makes happy living difficult. It's nearly impossible to enjoy yourself without respecting a natural process that enables new life to emerge.

23 September   *Be on time for every appointment.* Regardless of its importance, make sure you are not a minute late, even if you are certain, from past experience, that the person you are meeting will not be on time, or that the activity you are scheduled for, a doctor's appointment for instance, will not start at the appointed hour.

Prepare for the time you will be waiting. Make it an enjoyable experience. Bring something to read. Take a Walkman and listen to music, or better yet, just sit calmly and wait for the meeting or visit to begin.

Notice details of the room or area in which you're sitting. How does it make you feel? Is it friendly, or cold? Does it invite daydreaming, or do you find yourself feeling wary and protective? If you are waiting in a public building, how sincere was the person who greeted you? Was she solicitous or did she barely look up? Do you feel self-conscious waiting, or are you comfortable and relaxed? Do you find it easier to wait as the day wears on, or are you increasingly frustrated and irritated?

Think about whether you're usually on time, or whether you often make people wait for you.

24 September *Tell someone the story of "Little Red Riding Hood."* Fairy tales are not only for children. In fact, they represent some of the deepest unconscious feelings that we collectively feel. An unusual way to pass the time with someone, especially someone with whom you are struggling to come up with fresh topics of conversation, is to tell each other fairy tales.

It's said that the Duke and Duchess of Windsor, who lived in exile in Paris after his abdication, were sensitive to the press whenever they dined in public. Not wanting a reporter to get the notion that, after ten years, their relationship had soured because there was no longer anything to talk about, the duke and duchess told each other fairy tales to keep the conversation flowing.

If they're good enough for English royalty, they're good enough for you. Their simplicity is often revealing and can spark you to great discoveries about yourself, your partner or friend, and the entire human condition.

25 September *Play a board game.* Gather around you the people who would most enjoy this activity and set aside at least three hours to play something that draws out your skill, luck, level of teamwork, stamina, concentration, and ability to lose yourself in an atmosphere that you and your friends have created.

Have a marathon game of Monopoly. Pretend you are a child and re-create the hours you used to spend sitting around a board, throwing dice, moving markers, drawing cards, building hotels on Boardwalk.

Better yet, involve some children, and see how seriously they take the game. Play Clue, or Risk, or Candyland. The point is to create an entirely different reality, to leave aside the seriousness of the adult world for the playfully mysterious ways of childhood.

26 September *Organize a clash day.* This can be done at work or with a group of friends. But having a day where your clothes clash will engender a light, carefree feeling that will last for weeks.

The wilder the better. If you've been dying to wear polka dots but haven't mustered the courage, do it today—but make sure you combine them with madras plaid. See how creative you can be. Make your outfit into a costume. And the more people you can get to join you, the more fun you'll have.

Today is the day you can break the mold on your attire. Ignore convention. Put away that blue suit, white shirt, and red tie. Put on an outfit that will make people cringe. See if you can do it. See if you have the courage. What's the worst thing that can happen? If everyone around you is following the same course, then you're all normal. Right?

Get your whole family in on the fun and parade down the center of the mall. Notice the looks you get.

27 September   *Take a risk with your money.* Determine ahead of time how much you can safely afford to lose, put that money aside, and gamble with it. You can take a calculated risk by investing more funds than you normally would in a project at work, lending money to a friend for a business venture, or playing a sporting game. Even if your spending limit is five dollars, you'll still be able to have fun trying to increase that amount.

There are a number of ways to gamble legally. You can buy lottery tickets, but there's no skill involved in that. If you live close to Las Vegas, Atlantic City, or another place where gambling is legal, you can go to a casino, where you can play any number of games.

Or you can go to a racetrack and bet on the horses. Buy a copy of the *Racing Form*, study the horses' past performances, and place your bet.

Organize a poker game with your friends. Penny ante games are just as much fun as higher-stake ones.

Make sure you don't lose more than your pocketbook allows. Make an agreement with the other players to support your decision to drop out when you've reached your limit.

28 September *Think everything through before you act.* Do nothing today that you haven't thoroughly considered ahead of time.

What are the consequences of your actions? What results are you intending? What result might take place that you are not intending? Every move, every motion, every tiny reaction to any event has consequences. Make sure you are aware of them before you commit yourself to action.

Let's say you decide to kick a stone that's lying on the ground. Could you bruise or stub your toe? Might you fall, overshoot your mark, strain your leg? What if your kick is better than you think and the stone flies in the air? Are there cars around that could be scratched? Are there children nearby who could be hurt?

Make sure you know what you're doing when you act. And if you can't be aware of all the consequences, make sure you know that as well. The merger of thought and action informs and transforms both.

29 September   *Go on a boat ride.* For many people, moving at a decent speed in the water is one of the most satisfying feelings in life. If you live close to a river, bay, or lake, you should have no trouble finding a boat that will carry you from one spot to another.

Are you near a ferry? Hop on it. Drive your car onto the boat, get out, and feel the spray. Listen to the sounds that are heard only near the sea: the call of a sea gull, a foghorn, the roar of the boat's engine, the way the deckhands talk to one another, the clanking of metal as the gangway is lifted and dropped.

If a ferry is not accessible, go sailing or kayaking, or, if you can afford it, you might even consider setting sail on a cruise ship.

As you move through the water, regardless of the vessel, think about the joys of this particular mode of transportation, about how we moved around on water long before roads made overland travel possible and long before the airplane was invented. Most of the world's greatest cities are located on water.

One of mankind's first great dreams was to be able to sail the earth. Going on a boat ride puts you in touch with our ancestors' earliest desires, and enables you—as their progeny—to fulfill them.

30 September · *Make a wish upon a star.*

This is a great thing to do with a new lover, and there are ways to make the event really special.

Sunset is a delightful time to begin the festivities. Find a spot from which you can clearly see the sun go down. If you are close to a body of water, that's perfect, but high on a ridge, or in a clear field, is also good.

Of course the sky has to be cloudless. As the sun descends, look around for the first visible star. It should be in the western sky, near the setting sun.

Now make your wish. Some people say that wishes have to be silent, that they can't be revealed, but only you can make the rules. Ask the star to grant your wish. If your companion wants to make more than one wish, that's fine. In fact, you can allow one, two, three, or more wishes. Try to make only one wish per star, however, as all stars like to be asked to grant a request.

Watch the expression on your lover's face as he or she faces the star with closed eyes, and asks that his or her wish be granted with as much intensity as he or she can muster.

Do this as often as the mood strikes, or when you really want something to happen.

On Happiness and Self-Responsibility

You maximize your potential for happiness if you decide right now to accept responsibility for your life. The way you feel is what you have created, regardless of the influence or impact someone else may have on you.

It's a simple matter, really. It involves the notion that where you are right now, what you're doing, with whom you're doing it, regardless of the circumstances, is your choice. You have created your life, you continue to create it, and will always create it. If your life doesn't work for you, it's because you have not allowed yourself to believe that you can create a healthy, happy one.

It's amazing how much easier life is when you become one with your word. To say "yes" when you mean "yes," and "no" when you mean "no," and "maybe" when you mean "maybe," and "I don't know" when you mean "I don't know" may appear to be elementary, but you'd be surprised at how difficult it is for most people to do. The pressure to conform, to be pleasing or consistent with whatever image you have of yourself, is often overwhelming and difficult to resist. It becomes easier—and we learn this in early childhood—just to say whatever you think the other person wants to hear. Conflict or unpleasantness or confrontation is avoided.

By the time we're older, it has become a way of life. And it is also a burden. Following through on your word, keeping commitments, and taking responsibility for your actions frees you of many of life's difficulties, and—because you are not constantly thinking about the negative repercussions of what you did, didn't do, should have done, or feel guilty about—allows more time for rest, relaxation, and pleasure.

Inflexibly keeping on track is not the objective. Conditions change, and at times it is necessary to change with them. If you find that you have miscalculated the scope of a commitment, there is no shame in changing your mind about it, or taking as much time as you want, need, or have, to follow through on it. It's important, however, to communicate what has changed to all those involved so that you can still keep your commitment, which is an essential part of both mindfulness and happiness. There is little peace in irresponsibility.

October

1 *October* *Contribute to your favorite cause.*
Determine which is worthy of your help by figuring out what
is truly important to you. Many people are working this very
moment to try to advance your favorite idea, so find out
about them and donate to the organization at which they're
employed.

Make sure the amount you give is not enough to put you
in financial difficulty, but enough so that you know you've
made a substantial contribution—for *you*. This may be
$1,000, $100, or $1. The amount is not important. What is
important is its significance to your budget. Go just a little
farther than what you know you are comfortable giving.

With your check, enclose a little note thanking the people who work for your cause for their dedication, good deeds,
and sacrifice. Let them know you appreciate their efforts,
and that it makes you feel good to realize they're working to
accomplish something you deem vital.

2 *October* *Spend a prolonged period of time
with someone—at least a few hours—but do separate
things.* Experience the feeling of being so intimate with
another person that there is no need to interact constantly.

One of you can read a book while the other wraps a birthday gift. Or both of you can get immersed in different books.

One of you can snooze while the other catches up with correspondence, or writes in his or her journal.

Learning to be intimate with someone goes beyond the ability to be sexual, to share one's innermost feelings, and to be the focus of each other's attention. It also involves granting another person the freedom to be him- or herself in your presence. It means allowing the other person to live his or her own life knowing that your love includes and even honors this separateness.

3 *October   Have a conversation with a person from another country who is visiting or has recently moved here.* If someone is not readily available, try the following possibilities: a business acquaintance, a friend of a friend, or a merchant or salesperson.

Make sure you can find a common language that will enable you to get beyond subjects like the weather or the rate of currency exchange. And also make sure that this person's cultural reference is a foreign one, not someone who was born in Frankfurt but has lived in the United States for the past twenty years.

Try to learn the truth about this person, to pick out how you two are different, and also how you are similar. What are your counterpart's core beliefs? What is his or her world view? See if you can get to the assumptions underlying his or her culture.

Ask about this individual's experience of America and Americans. What does he or she like most about us? Least? See if you can get your acquaintance to open up and reveal his or her true feelings, to get past politeness and talk candidly about his or her views of American life and how we differ from other cultures.

4 October   *Spend the night in a hotel in your own hometown.* Experience your city as a visitor. Check in during the late afternoon, acting as if you've just arrived by train or plane from a very long distance. Unpack your bags and start to get a feel of the people who serve you in the hotel.

Do what you would do if you were a business traveler to your city, or vacationing there. Experience the familiarity of your living area through the eyes of a traveler.

If your budget doesn't allow for an evening in a hotel, trade houses or apartments with someone. Put yourself in completely different surroundings, with the knowledge that you have done so consciously. Become aware of all the actions you take, how automatic they normally are, and how you have to think about every one of them because your familiarity has been replaced by strangeness.

It's easy to shift your environment. You don't have to plan an elaborate vacation to derive the benefits of travel: the newness, the dislocation, the excitement, the exploration, the openness to strangers, and the immersion in another way of living.

5 October   *Role-play different people or characters with someone.* Act out a conversation or series of
actions in which you and your partner take on other per-
sonae. You can then switch with your partner (you become
her, she becomes you), or you can both adopt new roles.

As you play your role, how difficult or easy is it to be
someone else? Can you readily think of what to say and how
to respond, or is it particularly hard to speak as if you were
someone else?

If there are family issues that you feel need to be aired,
role-play with other members to understand the issues from
a different point of view. People can often open up when they
are acting as someone else and say things that can't be said
otherwise. If your teenager bridles at having to let you know
what time she intends to return home, trade roles with her.
Take her point of view and see how she reacts to it, and vice
versa.

Spend a set amount of time, such as twenty minutes,
doing this, and then talk about what transpired. You may be
hearing another viewpoint for the first time because you
actually had to verbalize it. Or, freed from the expectations
you face every day, you may find yourself in a position to be
more open, more receptive to possibilities and alternative
suggestions.

6 October *Start planning someone else's birthday.* Regardless of what year it is for your friend or relative, make it a special birthday. She doesn't have to be hitting the big 4-0, or the big 5-0. How about the big 3-4, or the big 6-2?

Ask this person to visualize a day in which everything she does is exactly what she wants to do, that she spends it with the people who mean the most to her, who love and understand her and want to celebrate her life with her. If her inclination is to go away for her birthday, start planning now. If there are special things she would like to receive as gifts, ask her to make a list, and let the people who usually get her something know what she'd like to receive.

If today is her birthday, it's not too late to make it a memorable one. Demonstrate your love by smoothing every rough edge for her today. Make all the calls. Handle the arrangements. Let her know how special she is.

7 October *Follow a common stock.* If you have absolutely no knowledge of the way the stock market works, this is a great opportunity to find out. There are a multitude of books on the subject, and *The Wall Street Journal Guide to Money and Markets* is one readable publication that will explain the basics to you.

Pretend that you are planning to invest a substantial sum of money in a stock and will have to choose one. Find out everything there is to know about the company. Many stockbrokers will gladly supply you with information, but see if you can uncover even more through business journals and conversations with people who are up-to-date on the market. Become an insider. Learn everything there is to know about the company, its performance, the predictions for its future, and what's written about it in the papers. It's also a good idea to check your intuition. Don't rely only on acquired information. Go beyond that to your intuitive side, which you are developing.

Pretend that you've made your investment and watch the stock for a year. How does it do? Does it go up or down relative to the rest of the market? What were the analysts' expectations of the industry as a whole?

At the end of the year, see how you've done. If you would have lost money, try to find out what went wrong. If you would have made money, perhaps next time you'll make an actual investment.

8 October   *Come up with a business idea.* Don't think about whether it's a good one right away, just let your mind play. Surely you've had moments when you said to yourself, "Why don't they have left-handed catcher's mitts, or rubber keys?"

Brainstorming business ideas is fun to do with someone else. Talk about the idea as if it's already a reality, as if you've got a company name and people have already heard about you.

Some of the factors to think about are: what is your product or service, how is your customer going to purchase and then receive it, who is your customer and where does he or she live, and how are you going to finance your idea? These are the basics.

Keep in mind that a lack of money is not a problem. There are many ways to finance a good business idea. Contrary to popular opinion, businesses don't go under because of lack of funds. Mostly they go under because of lack of creativity. Work within the funds you have, regardless of the specific amount, until you can bring in more.

When you have developed your ideas a bit, start writing them down. Begin a simple business plan. Every time you think you've improved upon your idea, work the changes into your plan. Keep looking at it and changing it until you feel you can start showing it to people. Then get their input and change it again. If you truly believe in your idea and can sell it to others, you're on your way to success.

9 October   *Watch a sporting event on television—with one small difference.* Turn off the sound. Experience the contest as a background to other things you could be doing. Your attention doesn't have to be riveted on the prattle of the announcers.

When you look at television without sound, it provides you with the opportunity to supply your own judgments about what is taking place. Also, you can interact with other people while the game is going on. You can have a conversation. You can read a book to your child. You can give your boyfriend or girlfriend a back rub. In fact, giving back rubs while you watch sports on television makes a lot of sense. The intensity of the action will really get your fingers and hands moving. A certain natural rhythm can develop between the action on the screen and the effort your body is putting out. And if your partner isn't fond of spectator sports, he or she will love them from now on.

10 *October*   *Take a picture of the same tree for the next three weeks.* Choose a tree whose colors are particularly vibrant—a bright gold aspen, a blazing red maple—and stand in the same spot every day when you snap your photos.

The best kind of film to use is color slide film. It shows colors with startling sharpness. The purpose is to see how change takes place in nature, how seemingly slow and imperceptible it is, yet how steady.

Each day's photo will look like the one you took the day before, but the difference between the first and last days will astonish you. At first your photo will be filled with vibrant color; then, after three weeks, there will be hardly any color at all.

The majority of nature's movements are agonizingly slow. This activity will demonstrate to you how difficult it is to "see" change, even while it's occurring.

11 October *Fast for a day.* See what it feels like not to eat or drink anything. Plan for your fast by eating normally the day before. Don't do anything differently. You might want to choose to fast on a day off, since not eating or drinking will put you in a contemplative frame of mind.

Monitor your sense of hunger as the day wears on. When do you feel most like giving up your fast? What does it feel like not to eat or drink? How bereft do you feel? Do you find yourself moving inward, becoming reflective and internal? Do you seem to have more time to do other things?

When you wake up the next day, eat a light breakfast, such as fresh fruit, or juice and yogurt—breaking a fast with heavy, hard-to-digest foods can be rough on your system.

Is there anything in particular that you learned from your fast? Was it easy or difficult to do? Did it raise issues that surprised you? Take this opportunity to become more aware of what you ingest.

12 October, Columbus Day *Think of the world as, to use Marshall McLuhan's term, a global*

village. Consider the international scope of today's particular event: Columbus was an Italian who was turned down on his request to sail west by the Portuguese and finally received funding from the Spanish.

Consider also that he sailed west, expecting to find India, and came across a land that had not been sighted by any but the indigenous populations (Leif Eriksson and the Vikings notwithstanding), thus touching off an era of exploration, colonization, and exploitation with which we are still coping.

Consider also that Columbus was nearly thrown overboard by his nervous crew, that he made four voyages, that he died a broken and destitute man, and that all this happened only five hundred years ago, a mere drop in the bucket of historical time.

Think of how easy, how varied, how nearly instantaneous it is to make contact with a place like Bangkok today. How is life different in the global village? What are the advantages and disadvantages? How much of an impact do events twelve thousand miles away have on your daily life? How has telecommunications affected the way you view reality? Think of how much the world has shrunk since that day in early 1492 when the *Niña,* the *Pinta,* and the *Santa María* set sail, and the day later in the year when land was first sighted.

13 *October*   *Memorize a poem.* Find a verse that is especially appealing to you. It could be the sentiment,

the vivid use of imagery, a sense of doom or of hope, that speaks to you. It may appeal to you in a way that you might not even understand.

Read the poem out loud to see how it sounds to hear yourself recite. Now start to memorize it, line by line. Memorize the first line to the point at which it just rolls off your tongue. Then go on to the second line, and continue putting two lines together until you have mastered the verse.

When memorizing, it's better to go back to the poem many times for short periods than to put in a lot of time infrequently. Ten minutes per day is better than one hour a week.

Recite the poem to someone special. Ask if he or she would like to hear what you've been working on, and stand up and enunciate clearly and with feeling. Then, when the mood strikes again, memorize more poetry. Some of my favorites are Rainer Maria Rilke's "Duino Elegies" and Lew Welch's "Ring of Bone."

14 October *Play the trust game.* There are a few ways to do this. One method is to blindfold yourself and stand in the middle of a circle of people. Have them be a foot apart from one another, gently passing you around. You can't see anything, so what you'll feel is the sensation of moving, falling, and then being caught and passed on again.

Another form of the trust game is (blindfolded again) to have someone lead you around. You are completely dependent on this person for your safety and well-being. Every move you make is guided by your designated navigator, who acts, literally, as your eyes.

How does it feel to be completely in the hands of others, to have no choice but to trust them? Can you get used to this idea easily? Is it something with which you are immediately comfortable, or does it take a leap of faith on your part? How well do you know your circle or navigator? Are they performing as you expected? Do you sense differences in the way each participant discharges his or her responsibility?

Trusting in something or someone outside yourself is a great way to develop your own instincts as well as feel a part of the whole.

15 October   *Conduct a spirited piece of music in your living room.* You can pretend it's a rehearsal and do this alone, or you can invite some guests to watch as you perform a stirring rendition of a familiar composition.

Choose something that can really get your adrenalin flowing. Put on Tchaikovsky's *1812 Overture,* Rossini's *William Tell* Overture, or Rimsky-Korsakov's *Scheherazade.* Be creative and energetic. Pick up a chopstick or a ruler and imagine yourself onstage, making the music come alive with your extravagant gestures.

Hear the music in your head as well as through your ears. Anticipate the crescendos, mute the parts that are softer, and try to *become* the music.

16 October   *Don't wear your glasses or contacts.* Experience the world without the benefit of corrective lenses, only as precisely as your actual vision allows. (Of course, do only what you can do without jeopardizing your health or the safety of those around you.)

What does it feel like to see—or not see—things differently? How do your other senses respond to the diminution of your sight? Do they start to compensate by providing you with better hearing, smelling, tasting, and feeling?

How much does it ultimately affect how you live to have your vision impaired? Is your life totally based on your corrective lenses, or do you find you can do more than you thought without them?

17 October   *Attend a talk on a topic of interest to you.* Check the listings in your local newspaper as to who is speaking in your area and plan to be there. The talk could be on the impact of the European Community on foreign trade, or how to flirt.

You can base your choice on the person speaking or the topic, but try to do a little research to find out who are considered the most dynamic speakers. People who are noted experts in their fields are not always the most interesting people to listen to, and other, lesser-known men and women can sometimes be positively inspiring.

When you attend the lecture—whether the topic is political, literary, artistic, or religious—pay more attention to the overall message than to every word the speaker utters. You might want to take notes to remember some of the points. How does the speaker sound? Is he or she convincing, or does the delivery betray some insecurity about the material? What feelings are engendered by the talk? If it is information you already know, see if you can still be open to hearing it in a fresh way. Does what you hear provide you with some insight into your life?

Check out the people in the audience. Is there a connection between the makeup of the group and the speaker's message? Does the audience—the people to whom the message appeals—lead you to see the information in a new light?

18 October   *Put away everything you use today.* See that all you do—making breakfast, going to work, doing your job, coming home, spending the evening—includes the disposition of everything you touched. Leave no crumbs, utensils, tools, clothes, towels, or equipment out. Put it all away.

Everything in your space, both at home and at work, should look like it did before you entered the scene. Wash, dry, and put away every dish and utensil you use when you're finished eating. File every document after you read it.

What did you do with the mail after you opened it? Did you read it, put away the things you need and throw away the rest, or is it still lying on the kitchen table? Did you use the Yellow Pages to call a store? Where is the book now? Back where you found it, I trust.

19 *October*   *Go dancing.* What is your taste in music? Is it Latin? Big band? Country and western? Disco? Ballroom? The minuet? Get some friends together and spend an evening on the dance floor.

When you arrive at the club or ballroom, you might want to take a few moments to feel the beat, to get comfortable, to order a drink or find a place where you and your party can sit. Then, when the mood strikes, or when you are asked, get up and hit the floor.

Make sure you stay long enough to work up a sweat. Request a song or two of the band or the DJ, and don't leave until you're genuinely tired.

Make the measure of your enjoyment the level of your exhaustion. Really go to the limit. Get pooped. Feel the workout, and the sense that you literally lost yourself in the music. Experience the excitement, the buzz of the crowd. If you need to take a breather, take a walk outside and then come back in for another round.

20 October   *Walk through the fallen leaves.*
Feel what it was like to be a kid, to be drawn to every pile of
dead leaves you encountered, to live to get into the next pile.

Walk home from work on a route that will take you
through as many leaves as possible, or make a special trip to
seek out leaves in your neighborhood. The point is to feel
that sensation of your feet getting lost in the pile, to hear the
sound of the dead leaves crinkling and crackling and crunch-
ing as they fly up and are crushed beneath your shoes.

Invite someone along, scoop up leaves, and throw them
on each other. See if you can bury your companion.

Count how many steps you take in the leaves. Take at
least a hundred. Make sure your shoes are scuffed and dirty
before you decide it's time to go home.

21 October   *Start an aquarium.* This is a
great way to experience animal life without the responsibility of caring for larger creatures. It's also an uncommon way
to see how varied nature is. You'll be amazed at how
attached you can become to your fish, how different their
personalities are, how much there is to learn about the various choices you can make.

There are many ways to set up your tank, depending on your budget and your ambition. A small tank with just a few fish can provide just as much pleasure as a large one. Kids love aquariums. It's a great way for them to see how marine life lives from day to day, to marvel at the colors that fish display, and to have the responsibility of taking care of something living that is well within their capabilities.

Although it can be a good place to start, there is much more to underwater life than a goldfish in a small fishbowl.

22 October   *Eat leftovers.* Prepare an entire meal with food you've already cooked, food that's frozen or sitting in your refrigerator, just waiting to be devoured. Put together a meal of odds and ends that would never appear in anyone's gourmet cookbook but has a logic and an appeal of its own.

Get out the rice from the Chinese food you had last night, combine it with the beans from the Mexican food you had two nights ago, and make this into an appetizer. Then move on to the soup from Aunt Gertie that you've frozen for months, waiting for the right moment and not knowing exactly what it would go with. The right moment has arrived.

For the main course, there are a few pieces of eggplant parmesan lurking behind the ice-cube trays, and they're aching to be part of this meal. Add anything you like that you don't have to prepare. This feast is totally put together as if you were part of a prehistoric hunting and gathering tribe and the field in which you must forage is your refrigerator.

For dessert, reach in for some apples and pears, open up a box of crackers, and pull out some cheese. You just completed a delicious meal that much of the world would envy, and it's all been catch as catch can.

23 October *Baby-sit for someone else's child.* Volunteer to watch an infant or toddler for an afternoon or evening, thereby giving the parents a much-needed break. What matters is that you recognize the gift you give someone when you offer to watch their child for a time, and how good it will make you feel to give that gift.

If you're going to sit in the evening, bring a good book or a video to watch. During an afternoon sit, the child will probably take a nap, so you might have some time to get work done, or write in your journal, or take a nap yourself.

When you're interacting with the baby or child, really be with him or her. Be responsive to her needs. Is the child hungry, thirsty, tired, soiled? Does he like to be talked to, played with, held, left alone? Tell the child, no matter what age, that you are going to be with him or her for a few hours until his mommy and daddy come home, and he or she should see this as a special time.

If you had fun, offer to baby-sit again on an anniversary or birthday, or on the spur of the moment when you get a hankering to spend time with this child again. Let the parents know how special their child is, even if you have to overlook unpleasant traits to come up with something nice to say.

24 *October*   *Write down your significant life moments.* You can go for as many as you'd like, but ten would be fine. These are the times that have stuck in your memory, which come back to you time and again, which never seem to vanish.

Sit quietly for a few moments. Don't try to think of these events immediately. Let them come to you. Ask your subconscious to bring to the surface the events and occasions that matter, that have molded and shaped you. Memories may come up right away, later in the day, in days to come, at night in your dreams, or when you least expect them.

Keep a list or diary of the events that have remained with you. Were you the one selected in the second grade to present a rose to the departing principal? Did you have a major pillow fight with your best friend when you were eight years old that seemed to last half the night and resulted in a broken bed? Did you have trouble sleeping the night you attended your first make out party, where you kissed the cousin of a boy in your eighth-grade class but never saw him again?

This is the stuff of which your inner life is made. The more you can bring to consciousness, the more you will know about yourself, and the happier you will be.

25 October *Practice some form of hand-eye coordination.* It's important that the action involves repetition, that you perform the same movement again and again until your eyes and hands begin to work in tandem, almost without your intervention.

Learn to juggle. You can start with two balls and just pass them back and forth before you graduate to a third. Even with two balls you will start to feel your body adjust to the activity. Or play with one of those small rubber balls that's attached to a wooden paddle. Play with this until you start to feel yourself instinctively knowing where the ball is going next.

Another suggestion is to lie on the floor on your back, and just throw a soft, small ball up in the air, catching it with either hand. Do this maybe one hundred times, and then try to catch it with your eyes closed. See if you can put your hand exactly where the object lands without looking at it. Practice this until you can catch the ball five times in a row.

Feel your body become an instrument of a form of communication that goes beyond your conscious participation. Do you feel yourself pass into another realm?

26 October *Give someone a back scratch or rub.* Ask someone to whom you feel close and who would particularly appreciate this bit of heaven if they'd like to experience your best back scratching or rubbing effort. Make sure you know this person well enough to put your hands directly on his or her skin.

Plan to be with the beneficiary of your generosity for about a half hour or more. You can do one or the other, or a combination of back rubbing and scratching. Tune into his mood. If he is silent, be silent with him. The choice is entirely his. If you're giving a massage, use body oil and make sure your hands are warm.

You may want to include a scalp rub in the process. Ask your partner directly. Tell him that you're warmed up and will gladly include a head rub or scratch in your offer.

The best rubs and scratches come from immersing yourself in the task. See your hands as a representation of your entire being. Ask your friend to tell you how it's going, whether it could be deeper, or softer, whether she likes long straight movements, or swirling circular motions.

When you're finished, cover your friend, darken the room, and ask him or her to lie quietly before getting up.

27 October   *Throw a food-tasting party.* This doesn't have to involve huge numbers of people, but more people will allow you to sample more foods.

This isn't a potluck dinner, the point of which usually is to eat a lot and spread out the effort and expense, but rather a way to evaluate different foods.

Ask several people to prepare a few dishes in the same category. You can make the main course, someone else can prepare salads, another person's responsible for appetizers, and still another desserts. The point here is to make very small amounts, just enough for a taste or two, but also to make a variety of dishes.

In the salad category, for instance, make a bean salad, a Caesar salad, a carrot salad, a mixed-green salad, and a *salade Niçoise.* Do the same for the other categories. For dessert, put together different pastries, breads and cheeses, a variety of puddings, and cookies.

It's important that you and the other participants refrain from making too much. This party is a way to taste without overeating, to sample foods as if you were at a food trade show or convention and you were a buyer for a giant food store.

See if you can eat this kind of meal without feeling stuffed. Little tastes can go a long way.

28 *October*   *Take a different route to work.* Whether you walk, drive, or use public transportation, make sure you get to your office or place of business by some means other than your usual one, even if it's just walking on the other side of the street.

If there's only one way to get there from your house, then sit in an unfamiliar spot, or read a different newspaper. Drink hot chocolate instead of coffee. Try to make your trip so different that you almost think you're starting a brand-new job.

By the time you arrive at work, you could be in a completely different frame of mind. Allow yourself to be open, sensitive, and aware of your environment like never before. See how it feels to be there, what your sensations are. Are you irritated, elated, disoriented? Stay with this feeling for as long as you can. Then watch your mood as it shifts.

29 October   *Donate blood to a blood bank.* If you are healthy, call for an appointment, and then set aside a few hours to relax and take it easy after you donate. The procedure is usually painless and the people who draw your blood are generally careful and solicitous.

Imagine the multitude of uses that might result from your generous donation. You are giving the very stuff of life. Your blood might save the life of a victim of an auto accident, plane crash, or natural disaster, aid in an esoteric operation, or be part of an organ transplant. Your blood may be used immediately, or it may await a specific purpose months in the future.

Giving blood and not knowing who will receive it is one very small, but very significant, example of the interconnectedness of all things. Part of you will eventually become part of someone else, independent of your choosing. All you do is make the choice to give; someone other than you decides who receives.

30 October *Visualize yourself being more creative.* Think about which skills or talents you've always wanted to develop. Do you want to sculpt, paint, play music, write, build things, organize groups? Whatever it is, imagine yourself doing it.

Sit quietly and see yourself already doing what your heart desires. If your passion is painting, see yourself in front of a blank canvas, your colors arrayed provocatively on your palette. Now watch as you begin to apply the paint. Whether you choose to paint something that exists, like a scene or a portrait, or you want to let the colors themselves create the composition, see yourself working steadily to complete the painting.

Can you imagine yourself doing this on a regular basis? What emotions arise in you when you think about your creative side this way? Are you frightened, or reluctant to admit that you have the capability to perform these tasks? Or are you confident that before long you could actually let the artist in you come out?

Over time, imagining yourself doing something often produces the same result as actually doing it. If you can see yourself writing an award-winning screenplay, or sculpting a voluptuous figure, you have a better chance of doing it than if you constantly say to yourself, "I can't do that. I'm good, but not that good." Yes, you are that good.

Write down your creative visualization, look at it several times a day, and in a matter of time you'll begin to act on it.

31 October, Halloween

Dress up as your fantasy character. You don't even have to go to a Halloween party to get into the spirit of the day, but getting together with others does help. Think about who you would like to be if you weren't you, and become that person by donning his or her garb.

Your costume will certainly appeal to all the kids who come by your house to trick-or-treat. They'll immediately recognize a kindred spirit underneath that adult demeanor. Better yet, dress up like your character and go to work in your costume. If you always wanted to be Errol Flynn, put a patch over one eye, a sword in your belt, a kerchief over your hair, and swashbuckle your way through the day.

Have you always wanted to be a Girl Scout leader? Today is your opportunity to dress up in a green shirt with patches on your sleeves and pop a small beanie on your head. How about Fidel Castro? Put a cigar in your mouth, get a gray beard, and walk around denouncing the duplicity of the United States. You can be anyone. It's up to you. Go wild.

Does Utopia Exist?

I wasted a good bit of my early life being unhappy, even miserable sometimes, waiting for society to cure itself of its myriad ills. It was almost a requirement of coming of age in the sixties to rail against authority and condemn the world at large for not doing away with injustice. While those injustices were—and still are—real, I now see that I projected my own inability to create happiness onto a society that can never create it for me.

As a graduate student in the seventies I was seduced by the notion of Utopia—the best of all possible worlds, a society that knows no pain, no hardship, no deprivation, and no injustice—and I linked my own ability to be happy with the fitful progress I saw being made toward a peaceful, just, healthy, clean, fair world. If only we could create heaven on earth, the line of reasoning went, humankind would consist of happy, fulfilled, extraordinary people— including me.

While I still treasure, applaud, and support all the work that is performed to create a better world, I now understand the difference between happiness and justice. Justice is societal, happiness individual. The two are not identical. The creation of a just world will not automatically yield fulfilled people, although it will help the process along; nor will a just world arise from political agitation devoid of mindfulness. The work that an individual does or does not do to become mindful, to create his or her own life, is done regardless of social conditions. These certainly influence decisions, outcomes, and possibilities, but they do not absolve the individual from the responsibility of his or her own choices.

And in fact, it's my opinion now that the eradication of the world's social ills is inextricably tied with the development of mindfulness among its inhabitants. We are all responsible for our common home. The answer is not to wait for Utopia, but to create it by becoming more mindful. Our communities and our world change for the better to the extent that we are fulfilled as individuals.

November

1 November *Visit a retreat center.* Organize a trip to a place that is set up for your relaxation, that allows you to be in whatever mood strikes you—quiet if you choose, expressive if that is your preference, or a combination of both.

How comfortable are you in an environment that supports self-discovery? Does it feel like a regular vacation, or are you unusually focused on your inner life? Does the atmosphere of the retreat center lend itself both to meditation and examination? Does it have waterfalls or mineral springs? Does it offer massage? Is it calm, peaceful, and serene?

Perhaps there are some issues in your life that need to be addressed. Sometimes the best way to deal with them is to be away from your daily routine. A retreat center is ideal for this purpose. Perhaps you also need to work with someone else on these issues. See if he or she can go along with you.

See the retreat center as a spot that can support your effort to deal with whatever is going on inside you. How does it feel to be away from your regular daily habits? Is it easy or difficult to see your life from a perspective of healing?

2 November *Write out your holiday shopping list.* It's not too soon. Sit down today and think about each person for whom you'd like to buy a gift, and perhaps what you'd like to give him or her. If you can't think of a specific

item for everyone on your list, think of a category of gift—book, clothing, perfume—and write that in.

Go over your budget and figure out exactly how much you can afford to spend this year. Be realistic. If you only have $150 to spend on ten gifts, resolve to get the job done within that amount.

Form a mental picture of each and every person as you think of prospective gifts. What would he or she like to receive? What would make him or her happy? Try to give what you think each individual would like. Or, if you're not that confident, ask him or her directly. Would your daughter like a lovely silk blouse, or a makeover, or a set of screwdrivers? The more you let yourself think about each person, the easier choosing a gift will become. You'll be walking down the street and you'll see the perfect gift staring at you in a shop window. Or someone will mention in conversation an item that's ideal for somebody on your list.

Holiday shopping can be a delight if you plan ahead, buy in advance, and know how much you want to spend.

3 November   *Use only things that are reusable.*
Don't throw anything away. See how close you can get to spending the entire day without generating a single piece of trash.

Use a cloth towel, not paper towels. Use a handkerchief, not tissues. As for toilet tissue, buy some that is made from recycled material.

If you go shopping at a supermarket, bring your own paper and plastic bags and buy items in bulk, or fresh fruits and vegetables that are loose. Write notes on the back side of paper that's already been written on, and drink water from the tap or a spring.

Observe the amount of trash you've saved in just one day by not wasting anything. How does it feel to conserve, to go places on foot or by bicycle instead of in a car? How does it feel to know that you've used the natural resources of the earth to support your life rather than squandering them on waste?

4 November *Organize a family reunion.* Don't wait for a wedding or confirmation or funeral to bring everyone together. There are distant relatives who haven't seen anyone in the family for years, and perhaps it's time to change that.

The date of the event is important, so this is going to take some planning. Talk to other members of your family to determine the best time and place to hold the reunion. It may have to be six months to a year from now, but as long as everyone knows when it will be, this should not be a problem.

Your reunion might benefit from a theme. Perhaps everyone could bring their five favorite pictures. Another suggestion is to have each person write a story about another family member and put it together in a book before you gather so that everyone can read it at the same time. A reunion is a way of reminding you of your roots, seeing where you came from and also how far you've traveled.

When the reunion finally arrives, see if you can spread the organizing duties around. People should feel free to come and go as they please. And make sure that you schedule a family picture, or even a family video.

One nice thought is to honor the oldest person in attendance, the youngest, the one who came from the greatest distance, and the person who did the most work, who organized the event. Acknowledge the diversity, the commonality, and the peculiarity of your family. Does it feel like a normal one, or is it unusual?

5 November   *Vote.* This may or may not be Election Day, but whenever it is, exercise your right to choose who governs you, how your money is spent, and how the policies that affect your life will be determined. Voting is sometimes taken for granted because it's not a right we've had to fight for and because it's become somewhat chic not to vote. Buck the trend.

Make sure you educate yourself about the candidates, the issues, the propositions, the bond measures, and anything else that is to be decided. Take the time to know both sides of every issue, in an attempt to be part of what Thomas Jefferson identified as the bulwark of democracy—an informed citizenry.

Discuss the political issues with people around you. Solicit their opinions. Even if they don't agree with you, ask them their rationale for the positions they hold. Try to find out what values underlie their philosophy, why there are differences in your respective views.

Turn your vote into an exercise of civic responsibility, not a chore. Feel the connection with people in other centuries, who developed the practice as a way of assuring themselves of a voice in their lives. Think about the struggles that others undergo to gain this privilege.

6 November　*Get a psychic reading.* There are a number of ways you can make contact with telekinetic forms of reality. And you don't even have to "believe" in it or take it seriously. You can see it as a form of entertainment, like going to a play or show.

What's important is to be open to the information, not to judge or dismiss it. If you are receptive to the possibility, chances are your experience of any form of psychic reading will be positive.

You can attend a table tipping; have someone read your palm, aura, or tarot cards; consult the *I Ching;* or have someone do your astrological chart or hold one of your personal items and give you a reading. Get a recommendation before you go. It probably won't work to walk into Madame Penelope's Parlor of Prophecy, put down five dollars, and watch her look into a crystal ball. Some psychics are serious, respected professionals and your task is to find one of them and see what a professional psychic reading is like.

After your reading, let its message stay with you for a while. Don't look at it as if it were a mathematical certainty. See how it feels to have your inner life explored by someone else. Consider the notion that reality goes beyond what can be comprehended by the five senses.

7 November   *Visit a nursery of newborns.* Go to a local hospital and look at the pediatric ward. Go down the rows and see what new life looks like, how fresh and innocent and without emotional complication it is.

Notice the care given to these babies. Do the hospital personnel walk around with the attitude that it's just another job, or are they cognizant of the angelic treasures with which they've been entrusted?

Let yourself think about the whole process of life. What kinds of feelings are brought up in you by these newborns? Do they look mostly alike, or are there distinct differences among them? Are some active or restless while others are passive or serene? Do some make eye contact with you as if they've known you all their lives, while others look as if their focus is far, far away? What do their feet and hands look like, so small yet so perfectly formed?

If you have children, see if you can conjure up the images of the time when your own kids were born, what they looked like when you first saw them, how they responded to you, what thoughts you had. What were your dreams for them? Are they mostly who you thought they would be? Has the process of parenting been an uplifting one, or something much more difficult than you imagined it to be?

8 November   *Update your knowledge of your chosen field.* Whatever it happens to be, take the time to learn something new about what you do.

Are you an architect? Take a course on designing structures specially engineered to withstand earthquakes, or read Vincent Scully's *Architecture: The Natural and the Man-Made.* Do you work in a print shop? Learn engraving, foil stamping, or desktop publishing. Take a course in bidding for jobs, a skill that might enable you to eventually open your own business.

No matter how much you know about a subject or field, there is always more to learn. Life is one unending classroom: you are the pupil, and everything that happens to you or that you choose to do is your teacher.

9 November   *Have a brainstorming session.* The subject matter is of absolutely no importance. You can sit down with your family and talk about how to keep your dog from barking, or get together with friends and talk about how to save the world, or have a meeting with your co-workers and talk about how to save the company from encroachment by a tough new competitor. The reason for getting together doesn't matter. What does matter is that you create a forum for ideas.

The best way to do that is to keep the agenda loose. Let the topics evolve out of the interests of the participants. Someone should be designated as the chairperson, but only to make sure the discussion does not become repetitive. Someone else should record everything.

The session could start with one of the participants saying, "What can we do to help kids learn better?" That comment could evolve into a lively session on our problems with education.

Don't censure or judge anyone's response or suggestion. Even the most farfetched idea should be taken seriously. Encourage an atmosphere in which people's minds can soar, in which they're able to contribute their best creative thinking. Make sure everyone is heard, and that only one person talks at a time.

When the session is over, have the designated scribe read back everyone's comments, and see where the consensus lies on everything that's been discussed. Better yet, see if the session has a unifying spirit. If it does, determine if it is one you had anticipated, or something entirely new.

10 November   *Support a local artist.* Conduct an informal survey or some research to see who is doing

the kind of art you like, whether it's woodworking, painting, printmaking, sculpture, or some other craft.

If your budget permits you to buy this artist's work, by all means do so. But there are other ways of supporting an artist, ones that are less expensive and perhaps even more valuable.

You can start by telling all your friends, acquaintances, and colleagues about the artist. Talk him or her up. Make sure everyone knows about your enthusiasm for his or her art. Encourage other people to see the artist's work and perhaps even purchase it. You can also encourage the owners of galleries in your area to display the work. And you can volunteer to help put on shows and to invite people to attend.

Most importantly, you can really solidify your status as a patron of the arts by continually encouraging the artist. Never let an opportunity go by to praise him, to tell him how inspiring or provocative or soothing his work is. If you have criticisms, be specific.

11 November, Veterans' Day

Think about the nature of war, and of warriors. What is it about war that attracts you? That repels you? That you think keeps it a part of the world agenda as an instrument of politics?

Did you play with guns and soldiers as a child? Was cowboys and Indians a game you enjoyed? Or were you a military nurse who offered solace to the soldiers wounded on the battlefield?

Is it mostly men who are in favor of war? Are some wars just and others unjust? Do you believe in the notion of your country, right or wrong? What feelings are evoked when you think or speak about war?

With interdependent economies, and citizens in one country connected by telecommunications with citizens in other countries, does war play a meaningful role in the modern world? And how much authority should we grant to leaders to take us into war?

What role have you played in war? Do you help to create a warlike atmosphere in your home or office? How can you personally create more peace in your life, and in the world?

12 November   *Bake a cake.* If this is something you already do, then bake a different kind of cake than you normally would, or teach someone else how to bake a cake.

If cake baking is something you rarely do, this is the time. Don't be intimidated by the perfect-looking desserts you find in restaurants, or by the wonderful pictures you see on cake boxes and on television. Just determine that you are going to bake the most delicious cake you can imagine, and you're going to do it from scratch.

Look at a few recipes and decide which cake fits both your mood and your palate. Keep imagining the cake emerging in its sweet perfection. Is chocolate your passion? Or do you find carrot cake the one that makes your mouth water?

Give yourself enough time to do this with love and affection. Slowly put together all the ingredients as indicated in the recipe. Keep in mind how delicious your cake will taste, how much pleasure you and the other people who eat it will have from your creation.

When the cake is ready to be served, decorate it to celebrate something, even if it's to celebrate the first cake you've baked since you were seven years old—or ever. Take in the aroma and eat each bite deliberately, with complete enjoyment. Guilt is not allowed to enter your mind. If it does, stop until you can feel good about what you're eating.

13 November   *Winterize your home.* Whether you live in a house or an apartment, take the necessary steps to make sure you are prepared for the cold.

If you live in an apartment, talk to your landlord about what needs to be done to make sure you're comfortable in the winter months. Are your windows tight, or is the north wind just itching to get in at the first possible moment?

If you live in a house, make sure the gutters are clean of debris. Gather up all fallen leaves and haul them away. Get enough wood to keep your fireplace or wood-burning stove going, and fill up on heating oil if you need to do so. Make sure your chimney is clean.

Get your sweaters out and put away your summer clothes. If there are things you know you won't wear next year, this is a great time to give them away. Lay down the carpets if you take them up when the weather turns warm.

Preparing for the cold months makes them seem less ominous, less threatening than they might ordinarily appear. If you plan for them now, you can declaw them.

14 November   *Play the blindfold smell game.* You'll need to enlist someone's help in this activity, but it will be a fun and fascinating experience for both of you.

While you are blindfolded, have your accomplice put a variety of substances in small containers. Your goal is to identify the substances by smelling them. Some suggestions are the following: nail polish, bubble gum, coffee, tea, perfume, paint, suntan lotion, and vanilla. There are an infinite number of possibilities, and the more varied and diverse the better.

The point here is to see how deeply you use your sense of smell. Without knowing what you are smelling, determine if you can identify the substances.

Then have your friend do the same thing. You can use the same things or try different ones. Do this again in a month or two and see if your sense of smell has improved, if you are able to recognize the scents more easily than before.

15 November   *Get dressed up and go out.*

Make this a day or evening when you pull out all the stops and really show the world how elegant you can be. It doesn't matter in the slightest what you do. Your plans can be as elaborate or as simple as you like. Going to a fancy hotel to have a coffee in the lobby will do just fine.

If you have a tuxedo, wear it. (Or rent one if you don't and your budget permits.) Or put on your loveliest evening dress and your best jewelry. Look like a million dollars.

You don't have to have an excuse to get dressed up. There doesn't have to be a wedding or some kind of formal affair. You can do it anytime. You can wear a tuxedo every day for a week if you'd like.

Getting dressed up and going out reminds you that there's more to life than work and everyday chores, and that you can sometimes turn the ordinary into the extraordinary merely by changing the packaging.

16 November   *Sell something in your house.*

Tupperware parties have been part of the scene for years, but there are a variety of other products—household goods, cosmetics, toys—that can be sold privately in your home.

Organize a lingerie party. See if anyone knows a representative in your area and invite your friends and neighbors to join you. This is often a good way to earn extra money since the host usually gets a percentage of the sales.

Make sure the items for sale fit the audience. There are different lines to suit the age and inclinations of the wearer. See if the sales representative will bring catalogues and even models to liven up the show. Make it a party. You and your guests don't have to spend more than your budget allows, especially if there are enough people to make the event profitable for the sales rep.

How does it feel to transact business in your home, to reverse the customary shopping arrangement and have everyone come to you? Do you feel more—or less—like buying? Is it easier to make decisions? Does the familiarity of your own home provide a safer context in which to spend? Is there group pressure?

Is it fun to turn business into a social event, the way it still is in many countries?

17 November   *Have a slumber party.* This works whether you do it with people you know very well, like families whose children play regularly with yours, or even with those you don't. One very unusual variation of this is to organize a reunion of your college roommates and combine it with a slumber party.

One night will do fine, but two would be even better. Obviously it will take a while for people to loosen up and feel comfortable with one another. If you spend a weekend together, you'll be able to let things evolve. There will not be the urge to cram your whole life story into one eight-hour marathon evening.

How does it feel to see these people again after all this time? In the case of former roommates, do you feel the same kind of closeness, or does it mostly feel strange to spend so much time with people you haven't seen in a while, people with whom you don't have this kind of relationship anymore?

Do you find yourself wanting to be elsewhere, or can you focus on this group right here and now? Can you create new memories together?

18 November *Subscribe to a magazine, and think about a subscription you can give to someone else.*

What are your interests and/or concerns? What subjects would you like to read about on a regular basis? Health? Cars or boats? Fashion? Politics? Do you want to receive a weekly, or a monthly? Go to the library or newsstand, pick up the magazines in the area you've chosen, and see what they look like.

If you're not sure which one you'd like, you can subscribe to several, receive a few issues, and then cancel the ones you don't want. Most publications will allow you to do that.

As you begin to receive your subscription, keep in mind that you don't have to read every issue from cover to cover.

Just read what interests you. There will be enough material in the next weeks and months to keep you occupied, but even a magazine that covers a subject you love will not handle all there is to know about the topic.

When it's time to renew, imagine your life without this publication. If you can, drop it. If you can't, sign up again.

19 November *Make a fool of yourself.* Forget about any sense of what you should be doing, what is off-limits as far as behavior is concerned, what you are sure will embarrass you. Go to the limit of what you think you can get away with, and then go beyond it.

If there is no way in the world you can be affectionate to your boss despite your appreciation for the great support he or she has given you, break through the barrier and give him or her a kiss on the cheek. Did you just win a huge case for your law firm? Get up on your desk with a bottle of champagne and do the Freddie.

The bounds of propriety are so much larger than we imagine. The world is a much safer place than we often think. Only by going past the limits, by stretching the possible, can we redefine what is and what is not acceptable. If you danced on your desk every day, you would be thought a little strange. By doing it once, you show others, and yourself, how delightful you are.

20 November *Attend a play or musical.* See what a live performance looks like in which people act, sing, or dance. See what talent and stage presence is all about.

After the show, think about how it felt to be in the presence of people performing. What kinds of emotions came forth as you watched fellow human beings put their entire selves out for you to see, to judge, to enjoy, to lose yourself in? Did you empathize with them? Have you ever performed yourself?

Did you feel the energy of the performers? Could you relate to their intention, to their devotion to their art and sense of purpose? What makes a good performance? A great performance? What separates the many ordinary performers from the few stars? What qualities or characteristics do they possess that seem to be natural? Or is talent not natural at all, but merely a matter of persistence and practice, of having put in the hours required to achieve success? Or could it be both?

21 November *Hang out in an airport.* Plan to stay there for at least an hour, maybe two, and take a good look at the people moving by. If you can go to an international terminal, so much the better.

As you sit, see if you can distinguish the business travelers from the vacationers. In what ways are they different? Do they carry their bags, or have they checked them in? Do they have smiles on their faces, or are they preparing for battle?

How do people pass the time waiting for an airplane to depart, or for their friends, colleagues, and loved ones to arrive? What kinds of publications do people read? What about the airport and airline personnel? Do they share the same sense of adventure and expectation as the travelers, or do they make it just like a job, with the same kind of nuisances and irritations as any other?

If you're feeling adventurous, try to strike up a conversation with someone who looks interesting, perhaps someone foreign. If you're really feeling bold, make up a persona. Be someone other than who you really are, from someplace else perhaps. Or bring your work with you and do it as you watch the show.

22 November   *Look through a book of photographs on one subject.* It could be on a particular person, a famous building, a city you love, a planet in the solar system, or your favorite animal. Make sure that the photos have been taken by different people, at different times of the day, and that some are in color and others in black and white.

Since this is the day President Kennedy was shot, a day many of us can never forget, a book of photographs of Kennedy and/or the Kennedy family is highly appropriate. Do any two pictures look the same, or does this man, who was photographed as much as anyone alive, appear different in every pose? Are some angles more flattering than others?

Do you have a passion for Rome? Sit down with a few books on the Eternal City. Do the pictures take you back to a past vacation, or show you what the city must be like if you have never been there? Are the close-ups and the panoramic shots consistent, or does one type tell one story and the other a quite different one?

Is any one glimpse into visual reality definitive, or are there any number of sides to it? Why is it said in magic tricks that the hand is quicker than the eye?

23 November   *Go house hunting.* Even if you are completely comfortable where you live and have no plans to change your home or apartment, pretend that you do, and visit some open houses. Don't make anyone go out of his way for you if you are not serious, but since an agent or owner is going to be waiting around all day anyway, you might as well go and enjoy yourself.

See how other people live, and what kinds of dwellings exist besides yours. Can you compare your living situation with the ones you see? Do other people have more clutter than you, or less? What do you think of their taste in furniture and decorating? Does this process give you new ideas for your home, or do you like the way you have chosen to live, the things with which you have decided to surround yourself?

Can you tell a book by its cover? Do houses that have what is called "curb appeal" usually have a charming interior as well, or is there really no connection between the outside and the inside? What do you think of the prices people are asking? Does it reflect a buyer's market or a seller's market? Are the real estate agents helpful and cooperative, or do they show little interest in answering your questions?

How does it feel to walk through someone else's house, to see their most intimate areas—their bedroom, bathroom, closets—and be well within your bounds? After wandering through a few homes, can you imagine transforming your own life and home?

24 November *Take a siesta.* Plan your day around a huge break in the afternoon, during which you can have a large, delicious meal, take a nap, make love, or read a great book, whatever you wish.

You can get just as much done today as you normally do. The only difference is that your day will be stretched out to accommodate your much-deserved break in the afternoon. Instead of working straight through to 5 or 6:00 P.M. with a skimpy little one-hour lunch break, stop at 1:00 for your siesta, and go back to work at 4 or 4:30 P.M. Then work until 8 P.M., after your relaxed, refreshing, sensual afternoon.

Pretend that you live in Italy or Spain, where the afternoon siesta is still an entrenched institution. You might also be interested to know that Italians, on average, live longer than people in other Western countries, and have the lowest suicide rate. It seems like they're having too good a time to leave.

Examine how you feel at 8:00, after your long day is over. Do you feel less tired than you thought you would?

25 November, Thanksgiving Day

Enjoy each and every morsel of food. If today isn't really Thanksgiving Day, then save this suggestion for the real thing. With an array of wonderful tastes and choices before you, see if you can be aware of each mouthful, each bite, each taste, and go through this special meal with an awareness of yourself, of food, of the planet, of the reason for the holiday, and of the fact that you're surrounded by the people in your life who mean the most to you.

See if the food can heighten, rather than dull, your senses. Eat enough to be satisfied—even overeat slightly if you feel so inclined—but do so with an awareness that does not let any feeling or emotion go by without notice.

If you are engaged in conversation, slow down your intake so that you remain aware of your eating. Take frequent breaks from the feast. Focus on the various tastes, the amazing array of textures, the way the food is presented, the different ages and orientations of the guests. If this meal is in your home, make sure you spare no effort to make it as memorable as you can.

If you're eating in someone else's house, go out of your way to thank and compliment your host. Show your appreciation by offering to help clean up after dinner.

26 November *Start reading a long novel.* Select a book at least five hundred pages long and enter a completely different world from the one you normally inhabit. If you've been meaning to reread *The Last of the Mohicans* ever since it stunned you in the eighth grade, now is the time.

Make sure you have no preconceived notions about how long it will take to finish the book. It's like life. You may have some days when you can read all day, other days when you can't read at all, and on most days you'll probably be able to read for just a short time.

Whether you decide to read a book you've never read before or reread an old favorite, make sure the book catches your attention and piques your interest. Give it some time, but if it doesn't grab you after a while, put it down. How long should you give it? Trust your judgment.

Get into the book. Literally climb into the pages. Become a character, or try to see if you can anticipate where the author is going with the story. Go slowly. Take your time. You're in another world, and you can stay there as long as you'd like.

27 November *Eat a salad with chopsticks.* You can use either the wooden or the plastic kind, or even one of each. There is no reason you have to limit your use of chopsticks to Chinese or Japanese food. Chopsticks are the perfect way to eat a salad. Each piece of vegetable is already bite-sized, and if you're adept at using this utensil, you can apply your talent at picking up pieces of chicken in black bean sauce to an ordinary salad.

There has never been a better time to try this little experiment. Though you ate consciously and deliberately on Thanksgiving, you probably still ate a lot. These implements allow you to slow down. Just a simple salad eaten with two chopsticks will demonstrate that many seemingly inextricable pairs, like chopsticks and Chinese food, are not an exclusive connection.

28 November *Listen to music using headphones.* If you don't own a pair, you have three options. You can buy a set (there are some relatively inexpensive models on the market), you can rent a pair for a day, or you can borrow a set from a friend, relative, or neighbor.

Putting on the headphones gets you extremely close to the music. Sometimes, if you close your eyes, you can go to a place where you feel as though you're hearing the music live. (This works especially well if you have a compact disc player, since there are no pops or skips to remind you that you're listening to recorded music.) It's as if you're actually there.

What does it sound like to listen to music that pours directly into your brain? Is it more vivid? Does it get to the deepest part of you, the irreducible core?

29 November *Don't kill anything.* Take this both literally and figuratively. This includes both insects and ideas, the latter whether they are generated by you or someone else.

Instead, nurture everything with which you come into contact, whether it's a spider or someone's essence. See nothing as inimical to you, but only as part of what was called in the Middle Ages the "Great Chain of Being."

Pledge to respect the rights and integrity of all sentient beings, all those creatures that have life. Recognize that they have as much right to be alive and prosper as you do, and that your self-interest is enhanced when you see yourself as one link in a chain that includes all creation.

30 November *Know when to quit.* The old adage about winners never quitting and quitters never winning is baloney. All winners have known when to give up, when to recognize temporary defeat, call it a day, and move on.

In fact, it's only by recognizing the difference between failure and temporary defeat that you can allow yourself to quit and not beat yourself up over it. Temporary defeat allows you to step back, to take stock of where you're at, to decide if something isn't working.

One way to free yourself from something in your life that is not in your best interest is to separate means and ends. If you're staying in your present work situation (means) to be comfortable (end), then you have to look at whether it provides you with the comfort you seek. If it does, then you are where you want to be. If it doesn't, then you have to change your present means—in effect, quit—as you still hold on to your end—comfort.

Learning when to quit—a job, living situation, relationship, life goal—frees you from staying with things that don't work for you, and makes room for something better. Make sure, however, that before moving on you learn what you were meant to learn from the situation you're leaving. Pay the price for quitting. Learn to avoid similar situations in the future.

Acting Out
of Love

One theory of reality holds that there are only two entities in the universe—love and fear—and that they govern everything. How does this relate to happiness? If your life is driven by fear, by a feeling of lack or want, by the primitive instinct to avoid danger, then it is truly difficult to build a life of happiness. If, on the other hand, what you do is guided by love, by a genuine desire to live your life intuitively, in accordance with what you think is your purpose, honoring your unique gifts and talents, then mindfulness and happiness will be yours in abundance.

This is what is meant by doing things for positive reasons, not negative ones. Acting with a grudge, a chip on your shoulder, with passive aggression, with suspicion and mistrust, with the idea of conquering, manipulating, or deceiving the other person, will not only ultimately fail, it will prevent *you* from feeling good about yourself, your life, your choices, and will not attract people and situations that are in your best interest. You will find yourself having to rely more and more on this negative life strategy because your loving thoughts, feelings, and abilities have atrophied.

Did you ever notice how some people seem to prosper and enjoy life to the fullest, while others are out of control and up to their elbows in alligators? Why is it that some people take risk after risk and it seems to be no big deal for them? If you ask the right questions, you'll find that their attitudes about life differ from the norm. They act out of love—doing things because they want to do them, not because they have to. They expect positive results—not that things will happen exactly the way they want them to, but that what does happen, appearances to the contrary notwithstanding, can be seen as being in their best interests; they have faith—they believe in themselves and are the masters of their own fate.

Happiness is an attitude, a perception, an interpretation. It is not a commodity, waiting to be purchased and appropriated. It is a way of living that is loving, open, flexible, and respectful of what life offers, regardless of expectations.

December

1 December *Look forward to the approach of strong or unusual weather.* Instead of griping when the days turn foul—snow, sleet, freezing rain, or rain with cold temperatures—see them as an exciting adventure, as a time when nature reminds you that she exists, that when it comes to the earth, it is her domain.

Even a severe cold spell can be the source of pleasure if you are prepared for it, if you act accordingly and bundle up against the cold and wind. Can you recognize that we all live on a small, spinning orb held on course by the force of gravity among the nearby heavenly bodies, and that its position in the universe is very powerful, but ultimately also very fragile?

See the changing weather as representative of all change. As the earth moves around the sun through the course of the year, the earth is tilted at an angle of twenty-three and a half degrees—which creates the seasons. Consider also that at one time the bulk of the planet was covered with ice, and that erupting volcanoes are manifestations of the active core of the earth. We, living our lives day to day, are as much a part of this universal system as the moon, a grain of sand, or the sweet smile on your child's face when he or she wakes up from a two-hour nap in the middle of the afternoon.

All phenomena—including bad weather—contribute to our experience of life. Don't discriminate. Enjoy the adventure.

2 December *Attend a trial.* It's part of the basic constitutional process that all courtrooms are open to the public. When you enter the courthouse, there will be a posted roster of the trials going on that day and the rooms in which they are being held. You can choose a civil or criminal proceeding, as you wish.

See if the actuality in any way resembles the trials you've seen on TV or in the movies. Make sure you bring something to read, in case there are lulls. Observe each of the participants—the judge, lawyers, defendant, plaintiff, court reporter, jury, guard. In whom does the power reside? Follow the testimony, the arguments, the way in which the respective attorneys lay out their cases. Is the language of the legal system easy to understand, or does it seem like something foreign?

Immerse yourself in the atmosphere of the trial. Try to predict the outcome. If it is a criminal case, see if you can imagine the defendant committing the crime of which he or she is accused. This man or woman may be facing a prison sentence. Put yourself in his or her position. What would you be thinking right now? What do you feel about your freedom? Is it precious to you, or something you don't think about that much?

Stay for the verdict. Do you agree with it? Is it fair? Does the sentence, in your view, match the crime? What does it mean when we say we are a nation of laws, and not of men and women? Is that enough to guarantee our rights?

3 December   *Feel your pain.* Whether it's emotional or physical, immerse yourself in it. As you've already read, it is not the enemy. Don't try to hide it, run away from it, pretend it isn't there, or act like it's happening to someone else. Feel it. Make sure you know what your body, and perhaps your soul, are telling you by hurting.

Pain is a vital part of the healing process. Pain lets you know that something is wrong, that there's a part of you that isn't working, and that therefore the whole of you isn't all it could be. To avoid pain is to avoid reality.

If it's physical pain, make sure you find out what's wrong. Often the most minor things hurt the most, and yet slight pain can mean big trouble. If your pain persists, do something about it. See a doctor. Your body doesn't lie.

If it's emotional or spiritual pain you feel, embrace it as much as you can. Find out what's making you hurt and deal with it, either with a professional, with friends and loved ones, or, if you prefer, by yourself. Read books by people who have experienced a similar pain. Realize that you are not alone, whatever it is you feel, that others have found the road to comfort before you.

4 December   *Write down everything you do.* For one day make a record of each and every interaction or transaction that takes place.

We often have a sense of ourselves being a certain way when in fact we are otherwise. By recording everything we do for a day, and then perhaps on other days, we can see if our view of ourselves corresponds to reality.

For this day, for example, my record would be as follows: Woke up, lay awake in bed for a few minutes planning my day, got up, went to the bathroom and took a shower, put on a blue sweat suit, turned on the computer, and wrote part of *How to Be Happier Day by Day*. That's it. Since it's 7:03 A.M., my list is pretty short, but by noon it will fill up a few pages: I'll make and eat breakfast, wake up my son, make his breakfast and pack his lunch, take him to school, and then return to the book.

I'm sometimes hard on myself for not getting enough done, for frittering away precious time. When I write down all that I do, I see that it's not the case, that I am usually enterprising and productive. In fact, my list occasionally helps me slow down.

Making changes in your life, which many people would like to do but don't know where to start, begins with knowing what your life already is. And recording the things that take up your time allows you to see it clearly, without illusion or distortion.

5 December   *Do what comes easily or naturally to you.* Act as if you are water, and follow the path of least resistance.

With water, some of it ends up stagnating in an out-of-the-way pool, some of it gets siphoned off to be drunk by animals or humans or to be used for cooking or washing, and some of it ends up in a much larger basin, where a number of other possibilities await it. Whatever the fate of each individual drop, water does not protest.

As with water, let your day flow from one activity to another. If you feel like talking on the telephone, then make as many calls as you desire, or wait and let other people call you. If your inclination is to perform simple tasks, like picking things up and putting them away, then putter around the house, clearing tables, desks, and other surfaces.

There is an activity or series of activities to suit any mood. It's merely a question of figuring out what comes naturally to you at any given moment, what your inner life says would nourish you. If you wish to observe people, sit on a park bench; if you wish to observe them in peace and solitude, spend time in a library, or a church. If you are tired, sleep. If you are aroused, make love.

6 December   *Create an ad.* You can focus your attention on an imaginary product or service (perhaps the product you came up with when you had your business idea), or a service that already exists and—in your opinion—needs help. Putting together an ad will improve your powers of persuasion and provide a simple marketing structure for your company—real or imagined.

Although producing a television commercial is a lot of fun, it's probably best to start out with a radio script, or an ad for a newspaper or magazine. Start with the question "Who am I trying to reach with my ad? Who do I think needs my product or service?" Once you've determined the market, figure out which of the major advertising media—print, radio, television—will best reach that group of people. You don't have to be perfect about it, just close.

Then consider the message. To what do you think the people who are your target audience would respond? This is what big-time advertisers ask themselves all the time, although in their case great sums of money are spent on research to find out what motivates their target audience. If your product is expensive, consider an appeal to the emotions, since people don't generally buy expensive items on reason. If your product is inexpensive and utilitarian, a rational appeal to practicality might work.

Now write the copy for your ad. The headline should draw the reader into the text, and it's best to have a graphic, an illustration or photo, to create interest. You don't have to sell the product in the ad, only create enough interest to prompt the reader to call for more information or walk into your store.

7 December *Ask off-the-wall questions.* The more bizarre, the better. Pretend that your level of curiosity has taken a strange turn, and you've just got to ask the

butcher why the stamp on meat indicating quality is in purple ink.

Get into the mindset of a child. Ask questions that you would never think of ordinarily. Ask your husband or wife how lasers work. Ask your girlfriend what she thinks about when she's putting on nail polish. Ask your mother if she would buy a ticket if there were excursions to the moon. Ask your boss who buys his socks, or your best friend if Halloween is celebrated in Sri Lanka.

Break the ice of normalcy that holds your life in place. Asking questions that come up during the day will do that. Sometimes just asking the question will provide you with information that you never really knew you needed.

See how many people get into the spirit with you, how many play along, and how many act like you're crazy. Regardless of the response, however, see if you have a new insight today, if something you never thought about is in fact quite noteworthy.

8 December   *Buy some clothes in a thrift store.* You can get new designer outfits at half price, or buy unusual jewelry or hats. You can find these shops in most communities. Thrift stores are an antidote to the premise that you have to have loads of money to dress stylishly. In fact, it's not true at all, as you will note when you enter these establishments. You'll see items at prices you never dreamed possible. Consignment stores are another way to shop for less. People who buy things, wear them once or twice, then give them up, have done you a great service if you end up with their castaways.

Do you have any resistance to this suggestion? Is this something you only imagined other people doing? What kind of people do you encounter when you enter the store? Are they more like you than you imagined?

There are many ways to handle a limited supply of cash. "Secondhand" stores are not what they used to be. With the explosion in both production and consumption over the past years, there are lots of great things floating around, just looking for a home that will welcome and appreciate them.

9 December   *Play in the snow.* If you live in a warm climate, plan a trip to a wintry one, especially if your children have never experienced snow. If you live in a cold climate or there is snow not far away in the hills or mountains, take a trip up there.

Do the obvious things like build a snowman, have a snowball fight, or tromp around in fresh snow and see how much of it you can mess up. Or find a hill and go sledding, or snow coasting. Wear protective clothing and take advantage of what nature offers you.

Or go on a sleigh ride, especially at a resort at night, through the quiet streets or lanes, the sound of the horses' hooves and the bells of the sleigh the only things you hear.

Pretend you are living in a different century, before the advent of motorized vehicles, and this is your customary manner of travel during the cold winter months.

Then cozy up in front of a roaring fire, with something hot to drink and someone dear to you close by, and see how it feels to counteract the elements you've just experienced.

10 December *Welcome a friend or new neighbor.* If you live in an apartment building, find out from the superintendent or manager who has just moved in, even if it's someone who lives on another floor. If you live in a house, acknowledge the arrival of a new person or family on your block. Keep an eye out for homes in your area into which people have just moved by keeping up with the FOR SALE signs. Notice moving trucks coming and going.

Visit your new neighbors alone, or as the head of an official welcoming committee. Put together a basket of necessities, like salt, bread, some mineral water, and perhaps a bottle of wine and some cheese, and introduce yourselves to this new family. Show them that they have made the right decision in moving into their house. Even if you rarely see them, the spirit of welcoming will linger for a long time.

Provide them with tips about the neighborhood, where to shop for groceries, for whom to ask in the local hardware store, what dry cleaner to avoid, and assure them that they can call you anytime to ask a question or find out where to get a good haircut.

Making a family feel that it is part of a community, however loosely defined that is, is a vital step in actually creating a community. Welcoming a new neighbor shows that, whatever else is going on in other places, this new family is part of an active, helping environment.

11 December   *Choose someone you know very well, perhaps your husband or wife, and pretend you've just met.* Arrange to rendezvous somewhere and casually meet each other for the first time. This suggestion can lead in a sexual direction, but it doesn't have to. The purpose is to see someone very familiar with fresh, playful eyes.

As your encounter progresses, see if you begin to feel the same way about this person as you normally do, or if you can actually sustain the feeling that you're meeting for the first time. How effective is he or she at revealing only a little of him or herself? How good are you at this?

Do you find yourself slipping back into familiar roles, or can you remain in character? Can you ask probing questions? See how far your partner will go in talking about his or her feelings. They could be about you, or about anything.

Allow yourselves to stay in these new roles for, if you can, the entire evening. Sometime later, discuss with your partner what it felt like to have feigned unfamiliarity, to have staged a meeting, and to have gone on to get to know each other. Have you managed to rekindle feelings of surprise, of wonderment, of passion?

12 December   *Redecorate your home.* Whether you live in a one-room apartment or a thirty-room mansion, add new elements to your environment. It doesn't have to be your entire living space, and it doesn't have to be a complete renovation. Making just one change can provide a completely different insight into your habitat.

Perhaps it's merely a matter of changing the color of the walls, or adding a lamp to a corner of your living room that appears a bit dim. Whatever your ideas, talk to other people about them and get feedback. Consult with a decorator, or ask a good friend whose opinion you trust to help refine your ideas.

Check your budget. Keep in mind that things tend to cost more than you initially think, so plan a bottom-line budget at the beginning and let it creep up later. Add a rug. Put a new cloth on your dining room table. Make simple curtains. A change in your living space can open up new ideas in other parts of your life. A new color or addition to your home can lead to bigger changes.

13 December   *Take a sauna, hot tub, or steam bath.* Counteract the cold weather outside by heating your body to the core. If you made this a part of your day when you pampered your body in March, do it again. If you didn't, now's the time.

Each of the three choices has merit. If you like the feel of water, try the hot tub. If you prefer tropical conditions, sit in the steam room. And if the dry heat of the desert appeals to you, go for the sauna.

Feel your muscles and bones expand as the heat works its way in. Watch the beads of sweat begin to appear and then trickle down your face and limbs. Notice the sounds, the smells, what everything feels like. You can try the Finnish method and alternate between hot and cold. Jump under a cold shower or take a plunge in a cold pool before returning to the heat. A few of these round-trips should utterly relax and rejuvenate you.

Stretch out for a while before returning to your normal activities. Or really treat yourself and get a massage. Chances are you won't feel the blustery cold when you go outdoors again today.

14 December *Respond promptly to every-one.* Spend the day ready to reply, whether it is to your business associates, friends, neighbors, or relatives, even if it's to say, "I don't know," or "Let me think about it and I'll get back to you."

Answer all your calls immediately. See your response as the completion of an interaction that remains uncompleted until you carry it out. Don't be daunted by your feeling that it is too early to make a decision about something. Let the other person know where you stand. This is especially true in work situations, whether with a co-worker, boss, or someone who works for you, or with your children, regardless of their age.

Honor and acknowledge a person's reaching out to you by responding to them. In that way you return the honor. You show your respect by replying immediately.

15 December *Begin a long-term project and work on it a little bit every day.* Decide today that you're going to learn how to speak French, or play the piano, or learn how to do calligraphy. Determine that you have no time limit for this, that you are going to work at it for as long as it takes—two years, five years, ten years—and that you will continue with it steadily, a little at a time.

If you can't work every day, that's fine. As long as you make a commitment to something long term, you can turn to it when you have the time; even fifteen minutes or a half hour four days a week will add up to significant progress after a while.

Don't evaluate your progress too often. Just take a few initial steps and periodically see how far you've gotten. A few minutes each day doesn't appear to be much, but it works better than applying a lot of energy in a burst of enthusiasm and then not doing anything for six months.

Instead, work consistently. Keep at it. Just when you think you're wasting your time, spinning your wheels, chances are you'll have a breakthrough. If you want to lose weight, commit yourself to new eating habits and stay with them, even if you see no major changes right away. Your body is laying the foundation for a new you. All you need to do is make the commitment. The rest will follow on its own.

16 December   *Look at the world from the highest point you can find.* If you live in a mountainous area, climb to the top of a peak. If you live in a city, go to the tallest building and look down on life going on below you.

How does this perspective appear to you? Can you see people? Can you make out familiar shapes and sights that now appear unfamiliar? Can you imagine what a bird watches? Do you see both vastness and smallness at the same time?

See if you can get high enough to view, at the horizon, the actual curvature of the earth, the slight bending that is the reality of the planet on which we live. Astronauts have reported profound spiritual experiences when they first saw the earth from space. See if you can get high enough to have one as well. From the heights, you can put the reality of your everyday life into perspective. Compare it to the grand sweep of nature, the enormity of the physical world.

17 December   *Prepare your home for the holidays.* Make it festive. If you haven't done so already, go out of your way to decorate the rooms so people will want to come and spend the holidays in them.

This is an activity you'll want to do with others. Get all kinds of holiday adornments that represent your faith—a tree, holly, wreaths, lights, menorah—and weave them into your domestic landscape.

Be especially attentive to smell. The sense of smell is one of the most powerful ones we possess, and filling your home with holiday aromas will instantly create a magical environment, one that will remind you of wonderful holidays past, too. Have some hot mulled cider or apple wine with cinnamon and cloves steaming on the stove to permeate your whole house with the flavor of the holidays. Or make potato latkes.

If people visit you this season, ask them to bring something to add to the festivities, like a decoration for the tree, some home-baked cookies, a song to sing or a record to play.

18 December   *Look through an art book.* Turn the pages slowly and look at the paintings and sculptures that are representative of specific periods.

Which period appeals to you? What makes you like it? Is it the subject matter, the composition, or the color? Do you like abstract works, still lifes, or portraits? Try to see why each of the paintings is considered a masterpiece. What do you think makes them so?

When you've decided which period you like best, you might go to a museum and spend a day studying it. Note the variety of styles contained within a specific period. Try to figure out why these painters or sculptors are lumped together. What makes an Impressionist an Impressionist, or a pre-Raphaelite a pre-Raphaelite?

Decide which particular artist pleases you among those in your favorite period. Then get a book on this artist and look at the broad sweep of his work. See the development from his youthful style to his mature later years. Did his artistry change much, or was there a consistency from beginning to end that is readily apparent? Think about the nature of the individual, of the privilege of delving into an inner life through its creation, how unusual and odd that is.

19 December   *Have your child invite a new friend over to your house.* Make it a very special event for your son or daughter. Ask him or her to extend the invitation, check with the parent of the invited youngster, and plan fun things for your child and his or her friend to do.

Make your guest feel like a member of your family. Go out of your way to extend a warm greeting, to ask about his or her life, and to grant the child's special requests, if possible. Also make sure your son or daughter feels the excitement, too, especially if he or she is not used to "entertaining."

It's important to initiate your children very early in life in the ways of being a good host, of developing a hospitable sensibility, of making people feel comfortable in your home. So much of what makes life lovely has to do with caring for other people, and having a place to which people want to come, in which they feel comfortable, can go a long way.

To enable your child to feel comfortable being a guest as well as a host, arrange for the visit to be reciprocated. If you don't have children, "adopt" one for the afternoon.

20 December *Do you drive to work?* If you do, do you pay a toll at a bridge or tunnel? If so, pay for the car behind you. Do you take public transportation? Pay for someone to ride with you—a perfect stranger, of course. If you don't have the opportunity to pay for someone on the way to work, buy someone an hour on a parking meter, or a person you've never met a cup of coffee and an English muffin.

When you share your wealth with a stranger in a strange way, it provides both of you with an unusual story to tell and increases the likelihood of your getting treated in return. It's one of the universal laws of abundance—what goes around comes around.

21 December *Do a ritual burning.* Although the winter solstice has frequently been a time when such ceremonies were carried out, forget about animal sacrifices. Instead, think about all the things you would like to be rid of in your life, of which you would gladly let go.

Write them down on a single piece of paper. Whatever it is that no longer works for you, whether you've held on to it for a day or a lifetime, write it down. You can say, for instance, "I am letting go of my fear of water, of other people, of success, and of snakes." Or, "I am letting go of having to get other people's approval of me, especially my parents'."

You may want to invite friends and family members to help you usher in the impending new year by getting rid of what doesn't work for each of you. If you have a fireplace, throw the sheet or sheets of paper in there, watch your fears burn, and recognize that, as of this moment, you are lighter, more free, more able to consciously create your life.

Can you now focus on making your life work for you without the impediments that you just transformed into dust?

22 December *Take a walk at night.* You would think nothing of doing this in the summer months. Try it now, when the conditions are nearly opposite of what they are in June, and the sensations completely different as well.

Oddly enough, wind is not much of a factor on winter nights, so the element you'll mostly have to contend with is cold. See if you can pretend that it's completely natural to be outdoors now, that the weather is totally conducive to a lovely night out. If you can find a place to ice-skate, even better.

What does winter feel like to you? What kind of emotions or memories of childhood does it evoke? If you can manage to walk in falling snow, do it. Immerse yourself in the experience of the elements, of cold, and inhospitable conditions, of the sense that you are alone in the face of nature's might, and that, regardless of the reality of your life at this very moment, you might be in a position to change all that by flying to the Caribbean or Hawaii.

Make sure you've dressed appropriately, that you take precautions and don't overstay your welcome in the cold, dark desolation of late December. Keep in mind, however, that despite the frigid conditions, the hours of sunlight are already lengthening.

23 December   *Try a different approach to parenting.* Whether your kids are six or sixteen or thirty-six, let them know you've decided to adopt a new attitude toward them, even if it's for only a day.

At this time of the year, when families are often together and tensions sometimes arise, see your child as an independent human being first and your son or daughter second. Deal with him or her as you would any other person, without feeling the need to be mother or father. Learn the important difference between caring for someone and taking care of someone, and focus on the former.

Ask your children what they want rather than assuming you know what's best for them. Find out what makes them tick, what motivates them to be their best, to be loving, to realize their potential. Be affectionate and concerned for their well-being, but also let them be.

Listen carefully to what they are telling you, to what they want from you, and try to provide it. Have no agenda. Just be with them, no matter who they are, no matter what it is they need at the moment.

24 December *Be easily awestruck.* For one day, be someone who finds everything wonderful, impressive, unbelievable. Make a fuss over the smallest achievement, the most insignificant development. Live today as if each moment contains within it the seeds of utter greatness.

At work, be bowled over by everyone's ideas, not in a patronizing way, but in a way that genuinely shows your high regard for their accomplishments, talent, and potential. At home, demonstrate your love and affection by praising your family members, by indicating through your words and actions how delighted you are to be their mother, father, brother, or daughter.

Act as if each idea you encounter today came directly out of the wellspring of genius, even if there remains a part of you that is unconvinced. See the beauty, the cleverness, the brilliance, in everything. Make this a day of revelation for yourself, and of support and encouragement for everyone around you.

25 December, Christmas Day

Give a unique gift to each family member or loved one by saying something special to him or her. Today is a day whose spirit you'll want to carry with you for an entire year, until next Christmas. If the holiday season means anything, it means the quiet, unquestioned acceptance of everyone's uniqueness and individuality.

Honor that individuality. Begin with your husband or wife or dear friend early in the morning, continue with your children later on, and call the people you want to connect with and express your joy that they're a part of your life. Let them know without a doubt how much you love them, how much they mean to you. You don't even have to say the words "I love you," although that would be great. All you have to do is let your feelings guide your actions, without reaching for the "perfect" thing to say or do.

Throughout the day, as you see, talk to, and spend time with the people who mean so much to you, take the time to be truly happy, to recognize that your life is your creation, and that what you have is uniquely yours.

26 December *Organize your bookshelves.*

Do you ever have the feeling that looking for a particular book is an all but futile enterprise, that what you really wanted for Christmas was a librarian to go through your books and put them in order? Well, you can do it yourself. It's easier than you think, and your system can be designed to suit your own particular sense of order.

First, if your books are in different parts of your house, put the subjects or categories that most interest you closest to where you spend the most time. Immediately, you know where your books are going to go geographically. Second, decide what categories of books you have and write them down. For example, your selections could be business, history, fiction, food, education. Now arrange your books alphabetically by author's last name and you have a functioning library that allows you to find books easily.

This is a great holiday project since there will probably both be people around who could help you, and the time to do it. Organizing your library will take less time than you think, your house will take on a completely different look, and your life will become more orderly.

If there are lots of books that you just don't care about anymore, box them up and take them to a secondhand bookstore, or give them to a charity. There's no need to keep them. Others may find just what they've been searching for among your cast-offs—if you give them the chance.

27 December *Do nothing.* Plan to do nothing. Make sure you do nothing. If anyone asks you what you're going to do today, tell them you're going to do nothing.

Have no plans, no appointments, no commitments, no obligations, no unfinished business or agenda. Today is a day on which you have no particular reason to get up, no calls to make, no one who wants a piece of your time or attention.

What do you end up doing? What is doing, anyway? What's the difference between doing and not doing? Let the moment rule today. In Zenlike fashion, do only what your mood or inclination tells you to do. As soon as you feel your energy start to fade, stop whatever it is you're doing and do something else. But at bottom, make sure whatever it is, it's nothing.

28 December *If you have an answering machine, change the message.* Now is the time to let the world know that you're examining every aspect of your life, in line with the coming of the new year, even the message you leave for the world when you're away.

See if you can spruce up what you say. Try to create a message that will induce those who call you to smile. You can tape the day's weather forecast, or a famous (or infamous) quote. You can get your kids to put together a thirty-second skit. You can all take turns saying something to overcome what is rapidly becoming a dearth of inspired messages.

If you don't have a machine, leave a creative message on someone else's machine, or suggest to someone how his or her message could be improved. We all encounter answering machines and go through the process of deciding whether to leave a message, what to say, and the frustration of not reaching the person you want to talk to.

Do something about that frustration by having your message be a little entertainment in your caller's day. Remember, you don't have to wait until next New Year's to change the message again.

29 December   *Play charades.* Get at least six people together, and make sure experienced players are teamed up with less experienced ones to make an interesting game.

You can use movie titles, book titles, or sayings. Act out each word in the title. The more dramatic the better. Let the ham in you out. See what it feels like to be onstage, to have all eyes on you, to have the responsibility of making people understand what you want to say to them through actions alone.

Charades often brings out the fun in everyone—even in people not known for their merriment. The more expressive you are, the more you'll feel a part of the group energy. It also helps to know some of the basic signals. But chances are someone in your group will know them.

Are you ready? Book title, two words, sounds like . . .

30 December　*Start to write a book or short story.* If you can write a best-seller, that's great, but keep in mind that writing and publishing any book is a long process. Realize right at the outset that you have to take it one step at a time.

What are you interested in? If you have a great imagination and you like to develop characters, try to write fiction, either short stories or a novel.

If you have an interest in a particular subject, jot down some ideas and begin to organize them. Get help. Enroll in a writing class or attend a lecture. The image of the hermit writer who doesn't talk to anyone about his or her work is a myth.

Have in mind a model of the book you want to write. Imagine the book completed, and people reading it on the subway, in their living rooms, or in a classroom. Just keep at it. Being able to write well comes from reading great books, and practice. You may have to write many stories before the one that is meant for everyone to read comes out. Or you might hit on the first try. Regardless of the outcome, writing offers you a splendid opportunity to organize your thoughts.

Make sure you know who will benefit from your book or short piece, the audience for which it is intended. And keep in mind what Gertrude Stein said: "One writes for oneself and strangers. . . ."

31 December   *Think about your purpose in life.* If you never thought about this before, or thought about it and decided you didn't have one, remember that everyone has a purpose, even if the difference between those who say they do and those who say they don't is merely a matter of recognition.

Have this question in mind as you go about your business today, getting ready for New Year's Eve and another year: "What is my purpose in life?" While it's a pretty broad question, after a while you'll start to come up with thoughts that resemble a direction, if not an answer. Just keep playing with the question as if it were a soccer ball that you kick all over the field.

Try to protect yourself from any premature conclusions. Let the question reside in you, be with you, permeate your being, and be transformed in the process.

You may decide your purpose is to show people how to live more joyfully, or help end world hunger, or bring people together for love. Try to narrow it down. Be as specific as possible. For instance, "My purpose is to show anyone that he or she can play the guitar," or "My purpose is to help athletes work through their injuries in a loving and gentle way."

Each individual is like no other, and the ups and downs, joys and sorrows, good and bad times, are so much more meaningful if they are placed in a larger context, one that partakes of purpose, of the sense that no other individual who has lived or ever will live can replicate your singular destiny.

Learning to Be Happy

In the best of all possible worlds (at least my version of it), kids would go to school and take courses in language and communication (both foreign and domestic), civics and history, natural sciences, mathematics, cultural subjects, and happiness. Each year, students would deepen their understanding of what it takes to be happy, which paths lead toward, and which lead away from, a life of fulfillment.

The point here is that you learn to be happy. Happiness is not something you're born with, although the capacity to be happy is innate, and your natural proclivity is to want to attain it. The difficulty comes when people don't recognize this, when they develop the feeling that some people have happiness and some people don't, and then give up trying to develop their ability to be happy because they imagine themselves to be members of the second group.

Happiness is deepened through practice, through discipline, through staying the course even when you don't feel that you're making much progress. Getting better at something is not a steady climb, like a rocket's. It usually involves great strides at the beginning, and then a slowing down, maybe even what feels like a standstill. This is when you find the going most difficult. It is natural to suspect that you've reached your limit, but be assured that striving to be even more mindful, even more happy, will produce greater results when the time is right.

If you are a parent, teacher, aunt or uncle, or grandparent, start right now with the children in your life. Teach them about happiness. Take the principles and suggestions in this book that seem to have merit to you and apply them in your mentoring or leadership role. Show your kids what true happiness means by living it, not just talking about it. The next time you suggest to them that you all dress properly and go out for a walk in the rain, or get in the car and go for a ride without a destination, they'll know something is different. And they'll love it.

I'd be delighted to know how any of these suggestions made you happier or more fulfilled, or what your impressions are after completing them. If you do other things that make you happy and would like to share them with others, please tell me about them. Also, if you want to know about happiness and mindfulness workshops and seminars in your area, send me your name, address, and phone number. Write to: Alan Epstein, P.O. Box 3011, San Anselmo, CA 94979.